UNLOCKING THE BIBLE

OLD TESTAMENT BOOK I

The Maker's Instructions

D1337617

UNLOCKING THE BIBLE

OLD TESTAMENT BOOK I

The Maker's Instructions

David Pawson

with Andy Peck

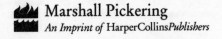

Marshall Pickering

An Imprint of HarperCollins*Publishers*

Marshall Pickering is an imprint of
HarperCollins*Religious*
Part of HarperCollins*Publishers*
77–85 Fulham Palace Road, London W6 8JB

First published in Great Britain in 1999
by HarperCollins*Religious*

1 3 5 7 9 10 8 6 4 2

A catalogue record for this book is
available from the British Library

ISBN 0 551 03186 7

Printed and bound in Great Britain by
Caledonian International Book Manufacturing Ltd, Glasgow

CONTENTS

INTRODUCTION

I suppose this all started in Arabia, in 1957. I was then a chaplain in the Royal Air Force, looking after the spiritual welfare of all those who were not C.E. (Church of England) or R.C. (Roman Catholic) but O.D. (other denominations – Methodist to Salvationist, Buddhist to atheist). I was responsible for a string of stations from the Red Sea to the Persian Gulf. In most there was not even a congregation to call a 'church', never mind a building.

In civilian life I had been a Methodist minister working anywhere from the Shetland Islands to the Thames Valley. In that denomination it was only necessary to prepare a few sermons each quarter, which were hawked around a 'circuit' of chapels. Mine had mostly been of the 'text' type (talking about a single verse) or the 'topic' type (talking about a single subject with many verses from all over the Bible). In both I was as guilty as any of taking texts out of context before I realized that chapter and verse numbers were neither inspired nor intended by God and had done immense damage to Scripture, not least by changing the meaning of 'text' from a whole book to a single sentence. The Bible had become a compendium of 'proof-texts', picked out at will and used to support almost anything a preacher wanted to say.

With a pocketful of sermons based on this questionable technique, I found myself in uniform, facing very different congregations – all male instead of the lifeboat-style gatherings I had been used to: women and children first. My meagre stock of messages soon ran out. Some of them had gone down like a lead balloon, especially in compulsory parade services in England before I was posted overseas.

So here I was in Aden, virtually starting a church from scratch, from the Permanent Staff and temporary National Servicemen of Her Majesty's youngest armed service. How could I get these men interested in the Christian faith and then committed to it?

Something (I would now say: Someone) prompted me to announce that I would give a series of talks over a few months, which would take us right through the Bible ('from Generation to Revolution'!).

It was to prove a voyage of discovery for all of us. The Bible became a new book when seen as a whole. To use a well-worn cliché, we had failed to see the wood for the trees. Now God's plan and purpose were unfolding in a fresh way. The men were getting something big enough to sink their teeth into. The thought of being part of a cosmic rescue was a powerful motivation. The Bible story was seen as both real and relevant.

Of course, my 'overview' was at that time quite simple, even naive. I felt like that American tourist who 'did' the British Museum in 20 minutes – and could have done it in 10 if he'd had his running shoes! We raced through the centuries, giving some books of the Bible little more than a passing glance.

But the results surpassed my expectations and set the course for the rest of my life and ministry. I had become a 'Bible teacher', albeit in embryo. My ambition to share the excitement of knowing the whole Bible became a passion.

When I returned to 'normal' church life, I resolved to take my congregation through the whole Bible in a decade (if they put up with me that long). This involved tackling about one 'chapter' at every service. This took a lot of time, both in preparation (an hour in the study for every 10 minutes in the pulpit) and delivery (45–50 minutes). The ratio was similar to that of cooking and eating a meal.

The effect of this systematic 'exposition' of Scripture confirmed its rightness. A real hunger for God's Word was revealed. People began to *come* from far and wide, 'to recharge their batteries' as some explained. Soon this traffic was reversed. Tape recordings, first prepared for the sick and housebound, now began to *go* far and wide, ultimately in hundreds of thousands to 120 countries. No one was more surprised than I.

Leaving Gold Hill in Buckinghamshire for Guildford in Surrey, I found myself sharing in the design and building of the Millmead Centre, which contained an ideal auditorium for continuing this teaching ministry. When it was opened, we decided to associate it with the whole Bible by reading it aloud right through without stopping. It took us 84 hours, from Sunday evening until Thursday morning, each person reading for 15 minutes before passing the Bible on to someone else. We used the 'Living' version, the easiest both to read and to listen to, with the heart as well as the mind.

We did not know what to expect, but the event seemed to capture the public imagination. Even the mayor wanted to take part and by sheer coincidence (or providence) found himself reading about a husband who was 'well known, for he sits in the council chamber with the other civic leaders'. He insisted on taking a copy home for his wife. Another lady dropped in on her way to see her solicitor about the legal termination of her marriage and found herself reading, 'I hate divorce, says the Lord'. She never went to the lawyer.

An aggregate of 2,000 people attended and bought half a ton of Bibles. Some came for half an hour and were still there hours later, muttering to themselves, 'Well, maybe just one more book and then I really must go.'

It was the first time many, including our most regular attenders, had ever heard a book of the Bible read straight through. In most churches only a few sentences are read each week and then not always consecutively. What other book would get anyone interested, much less excited, if treated in this way?

So on Sundays we worked through the whole Bible book by book. For the Bible is not one book, but many – in fact, it is a whole library (the word *biblia* in Latin and Greek is plural: 'books'). And not just many books, but many *kinds* of books – history, law, letters, songs, etc. It became necessary, when we had finished studying one book, and were starting on another, to begin with a special introduction covering very basic questions: What kind of book is this? When was it written? Who wrote it? Who was it written for? Above all, *why* was it written? The answer to that one provided the 'key' to unlock its message. Nothing in that book could be fully understood unless seen as part of the whole. The context of every 'text' was not just the paragraph or the section but fundamentally the whole book itself.

By now, I was becoming more widely known as a Bible teacher and was invited to colleges, conferences and conventions – at first in this country, but increasingly overseas, where tapes had opened doors and prepared the way. I enjoy meeting new people and seeing new places, but the novelty of sitting in a jumbo jet wears off in 10 minutes!

Everywhere I went I found the same eager desire to know God's Word. I praised God for the invention of recording cassettes which, unlike video systems, are standardized the world over. They were helping to plug a real hole in so many places.

There is so much successful evangelism but so little teaching ministry to stabilize, develop and mature converts.

I might have continued along these lines until the end of my active ministry, but the Lord had another surprise for me, which was the last link in the chain that led to the publication of these volumes.

In the early 1990s, Bernard Thompson, a friend pastoring a church in Wallingford, near Oxford, asked me to speak at a short series of united meetings with the aim of increasing interest in and knowledge of the Bible – an objective guaranteed to hook me!

I said I would come once a month and speak for three hours about one book in the Bible (with a coffee break in the middle!). In return, I asked those attending to read that book right through before and after my visit. During the following weeks preachers were to base their sermons and house groups their discussions on the same book. All this would hopefully mean familiarity at least with that one book.

My purpose was two-fold. On the one hand, to get people so interested in that book that they could hardly wait to read it. On the other hand, to give them enough insight and information so that when they did read it they would be excited by their ability to understand it. To help with both, I used pictures, charts, maps and models.

This approach really caught on. After just four months I was pressed to book dates for the next five years, to cover all 66 books! I laughingly declined, saying I might be in heaven long before then (in fact, I have rarely booked anything more than six months ahead, not wanting to mortgage the future, or presume that I have one). But the Lord had other plans and enabled me to complete the marathon.

Anchor Recordings (72, The Street, Kennington, Ashford, Kent TN24 9HS) have distributed my tapes for the last 20 years and when the Director, Jim Harris, heard the recordings of these meetings, he urged me to consider putting them on video. He arranged cameras and crew to come to High Leigh Conference Centre, its main hall 'converted' into a studio, for three days at a time, enabling 18 programmes to be made with an invited audience. It took another five years to complete this project, which was distributed under the title 'Unlocking the Bible'.

Now these videos are travelling around the world. They are being used in house groups, churches, colleges, the armed forces, gypsy camps, prisons and on cable television networks. During an extended visit to Malaysia, they were being snapped up at a rate of a thousand a week. They have infiltrated all six continents, including Antarctica!

More than one have called this my 'legacy to the church'. Certainly it is the fruit of many years' work. And I am now in my seventieth year on planet earth, though I do not think the Lord has finished with me yet. But I did think this particular task had reached its conclusion. I was mistaken.

HarperCollins approached me with a view to publishing this material in a series of volumes. For the last decade or so I had been writing books for other publishers, so was already convinced that this was a good means of spreading God's Word. Nevertheless, I had two huge reservations about this proposal which made me very hesitant. One was due to the way the material had been prepared and the other related to the way it had been delivered. I shall explain them in reverse order.

First, I have never written out in full any sermon, lecture or talk. I speak from notes, sometimes pages of them. I have been concerned about communication as much as content and intuitively knew that a full manuscript interrupts the rapport between speaker and audience, not least by diverting his eyes from the listeners. Speech that is more spontaneous can respond to reactions as well as express more emotions.

The result is that my speaking and writing styles are very different, each adapted to its own function. I enjoy listening to my tapes and can be deeply moved by myself. I am enthusiastic about reading one of my new publications, often telling my wife, 'This really *is* good stuff!' But when I read a transcript of what I have said, I am ashamed and even appalled. Such repetition of words and phrases! Such rambling, even incomplete sentences! Such a mixture of verb tenses, particularly past and present! Do I really abuse the Queen's English like this? The evidence is irrefutable.

I made it clear that I could not possibly contemplate writing out all this material in full. It has taken most of one lifetime anyway and I do not have another. True, transcripts of the talks had already been made, with a view to translating and dubbing the videos into other languages such as Spanish and Chinese. But the thought of these being printed as they were horrified me. Perhaps this is a final struggle with pride, but the contrast with my written books, over which I took such time and trouble, was more than I could bear.

I was assured that copy editors correct most grammatical blunders. But the main remedy proposed was to employ a 'ghostwriter' who was in tune with me and my ministry, to adapt the material for printing. An introduction to the person chosen, Andy Peck, gave me every confidence that he could do the job, even though the result would not be what I would have written – nor, for that matter, what he would have written himself.

I gave him all the notes, tapes, videos and transcripts, but these volumes are as much his work as mine. He has worked incredibly hard and I am deeply grateful to him for enabling me to reach many more with the truth that sets people free. If one gets a prophet's reward for merely giving the prophet a drink of water, I can only thank the Lord for the reward Andy will get for this immense labour of love.

Second, I have never kept careful records of my sources. This is partly because the Lord blessed me with a reasonably good memory for such things as quotations and illustrations and perhaps also because I have never used secretarial assistance.

Books have played a major role in my work – three tons of them, according to the last furniture remover we employed, filling two rooms and a garden shed. They are in three categories: those I have read, those I intend to read and those I will never read! They have been such a blessing to me and such a bane to my wife.

The largest section by far is filled with Bible commentaries. When preparing a Bible study, I have looked up all relevant writers, but only after I have prepared as much as I can on my own. Then I have both added to and corrected my efforts in the light of scholarly and devotional writings.

It would be impossible to name all those to whom I have been indebted. Like many others, I devoured William Barclay's *Daily Bible Readings* as soon as they were issued back in the 1950s. His knowledge of New Testament background and vocabulary was invaluable and his simple and clear style a model to follow, though I later came to question his 'liberal' interpretations. John Stott, Merill Tenney, Gordon Fee and William Hendrickson were among those who opened up the New Testament for me, while Alec Motyer, G. T. Wenham and Derek Kidner did the same for the Old. And time would fail to tell of Denney, Lightfoot, Nygren, Robinson, Adam Smith, Howard, Ellison, Mullen, Ladd, Atkinson, Green, Beasley-Murray, Snaith, Marshall, Morris, Pink and many many others. Nor must I forget two remarkable little books from the pens of women: *What the Bible is all about* by Henrietta Mears and *Christ in all the Scriptures* by A. M. Hodgkin. To have sat at their feet has been an inestimable privilege. I have always regarded a willingness to learn as one of the fundamental qualifications to be a teacher.

I soaked up all these sources like a sponge. I remembered so much of *what* I read, but could not easily recall *where* I had read it. This did not seem to matter too much when gathering material for preaching, since most of these writers were precisely aiming to help preachers and did not expect to be constantly quoted. Indeed, a sermon full of attributed quotations can be distracting, if not misinterpreted as name-dropping or indirectly claiming to be well read. As could my previous paragraph!

But printing, unlike preaching, is subject to copyright, since royalties are involved. And the fear of breaching this held me back from allowing any of my spoken ministry to be reproduced in print. It would be out of the question to trace back 40 years' scrounging and even if that were possible, the necessary footnotes and acknowledgements could double the size and price of these volumes.

The alternative was to deny access to this material for those who could most benefit from it, which my publisher persuaded me would be wrong. At least I was responsible for collecting and collating it all, but I dare to believe that there is sufficient original contribution to justify its release.

I can only offer an apology and my gratitude to all those whose studies I have plundered over the years, whether in small or large amounts, hoping they might see this as an example of that imitation which is the sincerest form of flattery. To use another quotation I read somewhere: 'Certain authors, speaking of their works, say "my book" ... They would do better to say "our book" ... because there is in them usually more of other people's than their own' (the original came from Pascal).

So here is 'our' book! I suppose I am what the French bluntly call a 'vulgarizer'. That is someone who takes what the academics teach and make it simple enough for the 'common' people to understand. I am content with that. As one old lady said to me, after I had expounded a quite profound passage of Scripture, 'You broke it up small enough for us to take it in.' I have, in fact, always aimed to so teach that a 12-year-old boy could understand and remember my message.

Some readers will be disappointed, even frustrated, with the paucity of text references, especially if they want to check me out! But their absence is intentional. God gave us his Word in books, but not in chapters and verses. That was the work of two bishops, French and Irish, centuries later. It became easier to find a 'text' and to ignore context. How many Christians who quote John 3:16 can recite verses 15 and 16? Many no longer 'search the scriptures'; they simply look them up (given the numbers). So I have followed the apostles' habit of naming the authors only – 'as Isaiah or David or Samuel said'. For example, the Bible says that God whistles. Where on earth does it say that? In the book of Isaiah. Whereabouts? Go and find out for yourself. Then you'll also find out when he did and why he did. And you'll have the satisfaction of having discovered all that by yourself.

One final word. Behind my hope that these introductions to the Bible books will help you to get to know and love them more than you did lies a much greater and deeper longing – that you will also come to know better and love more the subject of all the books, the Lord himself. I was deeply touched by the remark of someone who had watched all the videos within a matter of days: 'I know so much more about the Bible now, but the biggest thing was that I felt the heart of God as never before.'

What more could a Bible teacher ask? May you experience the same as you read these pages and join me in saying: Praise Father, Son and Holy Spirit.

J. David Pawson
Sherborne St John, 1999

Yes I thought I knew my Bible
Reading piecemeal, hit or miss
Now a part of John or Matthew
Then a bit of Genesis

Certain chapters of Isaiah
Certain psalms, the twenty-third.
First of Proverbs, twelfth of Romans
Yes, I thought I knew the Word

But I found that thorough reading
Was a different thing to do
And the way was unfamiliar
When I read my Bible through.

You who like to play at Bible
Dip and dabble here and there
Just before you kneel all weary
Yawning through a hurried prayer.

You who treat this crown of writings
As you treat no other book
Just a paragraph disjointed
Just a crude impatient look.

Try a worthier procedure
Try a broad and steady view;
You will kneel in awesome wonder
When you read the Bible through.

Author unknown

PART I

GENESIS

Introduction

The Bible is not one book, but many. The word 'Bible' comes from the plural word *biblia* which means 'library' in Latin. It consists of 66 separate books and is different from any other book of history in that it starts earlier and finishes later. Its first book, Genesis, starts at the beginning of the universe and its last, Revelation, describes the end of the world and beyond. The Bible is also unique because it is history written from God's point of view. A political history or a physical history of the universe has a focus determined by human interest, but in the Bible God selects what is important to him.

Themes

There are essentially two main themes in the Bible: what has gone wrong with our world and how it can be put right. Most agree that our world is not a good place to live in, that something has gone terribly wrong. The book of Genesis tells us exactly what the problem is, while the rest of the Bible tells us how God is going to put it right by rescuing sinful humanity from itself. The 66 books of the Bible form part of one great drama – what we might call the drama of redemption. The book of Genesis is vital because it introduces us to the stage, the cast and the plot of this great drama. Moreover, without the first few chapters of Genesis, the rest of the Bible would make little sense.

BEGINNINGS

The Hebrew title for this book is simply 'In the Beginning'. The Hebrew Scriptures were in the form of rolled-up scrolls and the name of each book was the first word or phrase written at the top of the scroll, visible to anyone seeking to identify which book it was.

When the Hebrew Old Testament was translated into Greek in about 250 BC, the translators changed the name of the first book to 'Genesis', which actually means 'origins' or 'beginning'. It is a very appropriate title as the book includes the origin of so much – our universe, the sun, moon and stars, planet earth. Here we have the origin of plants, birds, fish, animals, humans. We have too the beginning of sex, marriage and family life, the origin of civilization, government, culture (arts and sciences), sin, death, murder and war. We also have the first sacrifices, of both animals and humans. In short, we have a potted history of humanity. The first 11 chapters of Genesis could be called 'the prologue to the Bible'.

THE NEED FOR REVELATION

Genesis not only deals with origins, it also deals with the ultimate questions of life. Where did our universe come from? Why are we here? Why do we have to die?

It is immediately obvious that these questions cannot be answered by any human being. Historians record what people have seen or experienced in the past. Scientists observe what is observable now and suggest how things may have begun. But neither group can tell us why it all began and whether the universe as it exists now has any meaning. Philosophers can only guess at the answers. They speculate about the origin of evil and why there is so much suffering in the world, but they do not actually know. The only person who could really answer these questions for us is God himself.

Who wrote it?

When we open the book of Genesis, therefore, we are immediately faced with the question: Are we reading the results of human imagination or a book of divine inspiration?

The question can be answered by adopting an approach similar to that used in scientific enquiry. Science is based on steps of faith: a hypothesis is produced and then tested to see if it fits the facts. So science progresses with a series of leaps of faith, as theories are posited and action is taken based on the theories. Similarly, in order to read Genesis properly we must take a step of faith before we even open the book. We must assume that it is a book of divine inspiration and then see if the answers it gives fit the facts of life and the universe as we see them.

There are two clear facts in particular which are perfectly explained by the answers in Genesis. Fact number 1 is that we live in a wonderful world of magnificent beauty and extraordinary variety. Fact number 2 is that the world has been ruined by those who live in it. We are told that 100 different species are becoming extinct every day, and we are becoming increasingly conscious of the damaging effects which modern production has on our environment. Genesis perfectly explains why these two facts can be true, as we will see later.

The place of Genesis

Genesis is not just the first book, it is the *foundational* book for the whole Bible. Most, if not all, biblical truths are included here, at least in embryo. This book is the key that unlocks the rest of the Bible. We learn that there is one God, the creator of the universe. We are also told that of all the nations, Israel were the people chosen for blessing. Scholars call this 'the scandal of particularity', that of all the nations, Israel should be especially selected. This is a theme which runs through the Bible to the very last page.

The importance of Genesis is confirmed if we ask ourselves what the Bible would be like if it began with Exodus instead. If that were the case, we would be left wondering why we should be interested in a bunch of Jewish slaves in Egypt. Only if we had a particular academic interest in the subject would we read any further. It is only by reading Genesis that we understand the significance of these slaves as descendants of Abraham. God had made a covenant with Abraham promising that all nations would be blessed through his line. Knowing this, we can appreciate why God's preservation of these slaves is of interest as we see how his unfolding purposes are achieved.

What sort of literature is Genesis?

Many readers of Genesis are aware of the considerable debate about whether the book is God's revelation. Some have suggested that it is a book of myths with little historical basis. I would like to make three preliminary points concerning this.

1. The whole of the Old Testament is built on the book of Genesis, with many references throughout to characters such as Adam, Noah, Abraham and Jacob (known later as Israel). The New Testament also builds on the foundations which Genesis provides and quotes it far more than the Old Testament does. The first six chapters are all quoted in detail in the New Testament, and all eight major New Testament writers refer to the book of Genesis in some way.

2. Jesus himself settles all questions concerning its historicity by his frequent references to the characters of Genesis as real people and the events as real history. Jesus regarded the account of Noah and the Flood as an historical event. He also claimed to be a personal acquaintance of Abraham. John's Gospel records his words to the Jews: 'Your father Abraham rejoiced at the thought of seeing my day; he saw it and was glad.' Later he said, '...before Abraham was born I am.' John also reminds us in his Gospel that Jesus was there at the beginning of time. When Jesus was asked about divorce and remarriage, he referred his questioners to Genesis 2 and told them they would find the answer there. If Jesus believed that Genesis was true we have no reason to do otherwise.

3. The apostle Paul's theological understanding assumes that Genesis is historically true. In Romans 5 he contrasts Christ's obedience with Adam's disobedience, explaining the results in life for the believer. This point would have no meaning if Adam had not been a real historical figure.

If Genesis is not true, neither is the rest of the Bible

Such considerations do not have implications for Genesis alone. If we do not accept that Genesis is true, it follows that we cannot rely on the rest of the Bible. As we have already noted, so much of the Bible builds on the foundational truth in Genesis. If Genesis is not true, then 'chance' is our creator and the brute beasts are our ancestors. It is not surprising that this book has been more under attack than any other book in the entire Bible.

There are two prongs to the attack: one is scientific and the other spiritual. We will examine aspects of the scientific attack when we look at the contents of Genesis in more detail later.

For now we merely need to note the claim that many of the details included in the early chapters do not square with modern science – details such as the age of the earth, the origin of man, the extent of the Flood and the age of people before and after the Flood.

Behind the scientific attack, however, it is possible to discern a satanic attack. The devil hates most the two books in the Bible which describe his entrance and his undignified exit: Genesis and Revelation. He therefore likes to keep people from believing the early chapters of Genesis and the later chapters of Revelation. If he can persuade us that Genesis is myth and Revelation is mystery, then he knows he can go a long way towards destroying many people's faith.

How did Genesis come to be written?

Genesis is one of five books which form a unit in the Jewish Scriptures known either as the Pentateuch (*penta* means 'five') or the Torah (which means 'instruction'). The Jews believe that these five books together form the 'maker's instructions' for the world and so they read through them every year, taking a portion each week.

It has long been the tradition among Jews, Christians and even pagan historians that Moses wrote these five books and there seems to be no good reason to doubt it. By the time of Moses the alphabet had replaced the picture language which prevailed in Egypt and is still used in China and Japan today. Moses was university educated and so had the learning and the knowledge to compile these five books.

There are, however, two problems to consider if Moses wrote these five books.

PROBLEMS OVER MOSES' AUTHORSHIP

The first problem is quite minor. At the end of Deute...
Moses' death is recorded. It is a little unlikely that he wrote
that part! Joshua probably added a note about it at the end of
the five books to round off the story.

The second, and major, problem is that the book of
Genesis ends about 300 years before Moses was born. He
would have no problem writing the books of Exodus,
Leviticus, Numbers and Deuteronomy, since he lived through
the events they record. But how could he have obtained his
material for the book of Genesis?

The problem is easily overcome, however. Studies made
of people in non-book cultures have revealed that those who
cannot write have phenomenal memories. Tribes which have
no writing learn their history through the stories passed on
around the camp fire. This oral tradition is very strong in
primitive communities and would have been so among the
Hebrews, especially when they became slaves in Egypt and
wanted their children to know who they were and where they
had come from.

There are two kinds of history normally passed down in
this memory form. One is the genealogy, since their family tree
gives people an identity. There are many genealogies in
Genesis, with the phrase 'these are the generations of' (or
'these are the sons of' in some translations) coming 10 times.
The other is the saga or hero story – telling of the great deeds
which ancestors accomplished. Genesis is composed almost
entirely of these two aspects of history: stories about great
heroes interspersed with family trees. With this in mind, it is
easy to see how the book was composed from memories which
Moses gleaned from the slaves in Egypt.

Nonetheless, this does not answer all the questions about
Moses' authorship. There is one part of Genesis which he

could not possibly have picked up that way, and that is the first chapter (or rather 1:1 through to 2:3, since the chapter division is in the wrong place). How did Moses compose the chapter detailing the creation of the world?

It is at this point that we must exercise faith. Psalm 103 refers to God making his ways known through Moses, including the creation narrative. It is one of the few parts of the Bible that must have been dictated directly by God and taken down by man, just as God clearly tells John what to write in Revelation when describing the end of the world. Usually God inspired the writers to use their own temperament, memory, insight and outlook to shape his Word (as with Moses in the rest of Genesis), and he so overruled by the inspiration of his Spirit that what resulted was what he wanted written. But he gave the story of creation in direct revelation.

A confirming detail is provided when we consider that there was no record of the Sabbath being observed before the time of Moses. We do not read that taking a day for Sabbath rest was part of the lifestyle of any of the patriarchs. Indeed, there is no trace at all of the concept of a seven-day week. Any time references are to months and years. Since we have Genesis 1 at the beginning of our Bible, we assume quite wrongly that Adam knew about it and observed a Sabbath as a model to everyone after him. But it seems instead that Adam looked after the Garden of Eden *every* day and had time with the Lord in the evenings. Likewise there is no suggestion that Abraham, Isaac or Jacob took a Sabbath, and their work as herdsmen probably offered little time for rest.

All this need not surprise us if, as suggested above, Moses received the first chapter – including the concept of Sabbath rest – from God himself. With this knowledge, he was then able to introduce the Sabbath concept into the life of Israel through the Ten Commandments.

To summarize, then, Genesis is clearly a book from God
and should be read with this assumption. It is also a book written by Moses, using his education and gift for writing from his
time in Egypt to record the extraordinary works of God as he
reverses the effects of the Fall in the call of Abraham.

The shape of Genesis

It is instructive to note the overall shape of the book. The first
quarter (Chapters 1–11) forms a distinct unit, covering many
centuries and the growth and spread of nations throughout the
'Fertile Crescent' (the land stretching from Egypt to the
Persian Gulf in the Middle East). The watershed comes with
God's call of Abraham in Chapter 12. The next three-quarters
of the book has a narrower focus, chronicling God's dealings
with Abraham and his descendants, Isaac, Jacob and Joseph.

There are other divisions within this overall shape. In
Chapters 1–2 everything is described as good, including
human beings. In Chapters 3–11 we see the origin and results
of sin as man drifts spiritually and physically away from Eden.
We see God's character, his justice in punishing man, and his
merciful provision even within this punishment.

In Chapters 12–36 six men are contrasted: Abraham
with Lot, Isaac (child of promise) with Ishmael (child of flesh),
and Jacob with Esau. We are faced with two kinds of people
and asked which we identify with. God is tying his own reputation to three men, Abraham, Isaac and Jacob, flawed as they
are. Finally the text focuses on Joseph, an altogether different
character. We will see later how and why he is so distinct from
his forefathers.

In the beginning God

Let us turn now to the book itself and to the amazing chapter with which it opens. It begins with the words, 'In the beginning God'.

Genesis is full of beginnings, but it is clear that God himself does not begin here. God is already there when the Bible opens, for he was already there when the universe came to be. Philosophical questions concerning where God came from are really non-questions. There had to be an eternal something or someone before the universe existed and the Bible is clear that this person is God. It is the fundamental assumption of the Bible that God exists eternally, that he has always been there, that he will always be there, and that he is the God who is. His very name, 'Yahweh', is a participle of the Hebrew verb 'to be'. An English word which conveys the nature of God contained in the word 'Yahweh' is 'always': he has always been who he is and will always be just the same.

While we do not need to explain the existence of God, we do need to explain the existence of everything else. This is the very opposite of modern thinking, which looks around at what is there and assumes that we need to prove the existence of God. The Bible comes at the question from the other direction and says that God was always there and we have to explain now why anything else is there.

Certainly when Moses was writing, every Hebrew knew that God existed. He had rescued his people out of Egypt, divided the Red Sea and drowned the Egyptian army, so their personal experience told them that God was there. Further 'proof' was unnecessary.

The need for faith

The New Testament suggests a useful approach to considering God which will help us in our reading of Genesis. In Hebrews 11 we read two things about creation. First that it is 'by faith we understand that the universe was formed at God's command, so that what is seen was not made out of what was visible'. Then, a little later in the same chapter, we read that 'anyone who comes to him must believe that he exists and that he rewards those who earnestly seek him'.

As far as the whole Bible is concerned, therefore – including Genesis – we must assume God is there and that he wants us to find him, know him, love him and serve him. Then we see what happens on the basis of this trust. We cannot *prove* whether God exists or not, but we can hold the basic belief that God wants us to know him and have faith in him.

A picture of the creator

Moving on from the first four words of the book, we come to a feature that may be surprising: the subject of Genesis 1 is not *creation* but *the creator*. It is not primarily about *how* our world came to be, but about *who* made it come to be. In fact, in just 31 verses the word 'God' appears 35 times, as if to underline that this is all about him. It is not so much the story of creation as a picture of the creator. So what does this picture tell us?

1. GOD IS PERSONAL

Genesis 1 depicts a personal God. He has a heart that feels. He has a mind that thinks and can speak his thoughts. He has a will and makes decisions and sticks to them. All this forms what we know as a personality. God is not an it, God is a *he*. He is a full person with feelings, thoughts and motives like us.

2. GOD IS POWERFUL

It is quite evident that if God can speak things into being by his Word, he must be enormously powerful. In all he gives 10 'commandments' in the first chapter, and every one is fulfilled just as he desires.

3. GOD IS UNCREATED

We have already noted that God is and always was there. He was always the Creator, never a creature.

4. GOD IS CREATIVE

What an imagination he must have! What an artist! Six thousand varieties of beetle. No two blades of grass the same. No two snowflakes. No two clouds. No two grains of sand. No two stars. An astonishing variety, yet in harmony. It is a uni-verse.

5. GOD IS ORDERLY

There is a symmetry in his work of creation, as we shall see. The fact that creation is mathematical has made science possible.

6. GOD IS SINGULAR

The verbs in Genesis 1, from 'created' onwards, are all singular.

7. GOD IS PLURAL

The word used for 'God' is not the singular *El*, but the plural *Elohim*, which means three or more 'gods'. So the very first sentence in the Bible, using a plural noun with a singular verb, is grammatically wrong but theologically right, hinting at a God who is 'Three-in-one'.

8. GOD IS GOOD

Therefore all his work is 'good' and he pronounces human beings as his best, his masterprice, 'very good'. Furthermore,

he wants to be good to all his creation, to 'bless' it. His goodness sets the standard for all goodness.

9. GOD IS LIVING

He is active in the world of time and space.

10. GOD IS A COMMUNICATOR

He speaks to creation and the creatures within it. In particular
he wants to relate to human beings.

11. GOD IS LIKE US

We are made in his image, so we must be in some ways like
him and he must be like us.

12. GOD IS UNLIKE US

He can 'create' out of nothing (*ex nihilo*), whereas we can only
'make' something out of something else. We are 'manufac-
turers'; he is the only Creator.

13. GOD IS INDEPENDENT

God is never identified with his creation. There is a distinction
between creator and creation from the very beginning. The
New Age movement confuses this idea by suggesting that
somehow 'god' is part of us. But the creator is separate from
his creation. He can take a day off and be quite apart from all
that he has made. We must never identify him with what he
has made. To worship his creation is idolatry. To worship the
creator is the truth.

Philosophies challenged

If we accept the truth of Genesis 1, then a number of alternative
viewpoints about God are automatically ruled out. These viewpoints could also be called philosophies (the word 'philosophy'

means 'love of wisdom'). Everyone has their own way of looking at the world, whether they consciously think about it or not.

If you believe Genesis, the following philosophies will not stand.

1. **Atheism**. Atheists believe there is no God. Genesis 1 confirms there is.
2. **Agnosticism**. Agnostics say they do not know whether there is a God or not. Genesis 1 says we accept that there is.
3. **Animism**. This is the belief that many spirits control the world – spirits of rivers, spirits of mountains, etc. Genesis 1 asserts that God created and controls the world.
4. **Polytheism**. Polytheists believe there are many gods. Hindus would be in this category. Genesis 1 states there is just one.
5. **Dualism**. This is the belief that there are two gods, one good and one bad, with the good god responsible for the good things that happen and the bad god for the bad things. Genesis 1 asserts that there is just one God, who is good.
6. **Monotheism**. This is the belief of Judaism and Islam – that there is one God, and just one person, thus rejecting God as a trinity. By using the word *Elohim* to describe God, Genesis 1 tells us that there is one God in three persons.
7. **Deism**. Deists see God as the creator, but argue that he cannot now control what he has created. He is like a watchmaker who has wound up the world and lets it run on its own laws. As such God never intervenes in his world, and miracles are impossible. Many Christians are, for all practical purposes, deists.
8. **Theism**. Theists believe that God not only created the world but is also in control of everything and everyone he

has made. Theism is one step towards the biblical philosophy, but does not in fact go far enough.

9. **Existentialism**. This is a popular philosophy today, where experience is believed to be God. Our choices and our own affirmation of ourselves is the 'religion' followed. There is no creator as in Genesis 1 to whom we have to give an account.

10. **Humanism**. Humanists reject the concept of a god outside the created world. Although Genesis 1 tells us that man is created by God, humanists believe that man is God.

11. **Rationalism**. Rationalists believe that our own reason is God, rejecting the indication in Genesis that the powers of reason were given when God created man in his image.

12. **Materialism**. Materialists believe that only matter is real and do not accept anyone or anything they cannot see for themselves.

13. **Mysticism**. In contrast to materialism, mystics believe that only spirit is real.

14. **Monism**. This philosophy underpins much of the New Age movement. It holds that matter and spirit are essentially one and the same thing. The idea of God as an independent spirit creating the world is thus ruled out of court.

15. **Pantheism**. This idea is similar to monism, in that everything is believed to be God. A modern version of it is called Panentheism: God in everything.

In contrast to all these philosophies, the biblical viewpoint could be called **Triunetheism**: God is three in one, creator and controller of the universe. This is the biblical way of thinking which comes right out of Genesis 1 and continues through to the last chapter of Revelation.

Style

Let us move on to look more closely at the text of Genesis 1 and in particular the style of the chapter. The obvious point to make is that it is not written in scientific language. Many people seem to approach the chapter expecting the detail of a scientific textbook. Instead it is written very simply, so that every generation can understand it, whatever the standard of their scientific learning.

The account uses only very simple categories. Vegetation is divided into three groups: grass, plants and trees. Animal life also has three categories: domesticated animals, animals hunted for food and wild animals. These simple classifications are understood by everybody everywhere.

WORDS

This simple style is also demonstrated in the words used. There are only 76 separate root words in the whole of Genesis 1. Furthermore, every one of those words is to be found in every language on earth, which means that Genesis 1 is the easiest chapter to translate in the whole Bible.

Every writer has to ask about the potential audience for their work. God wanted the story of creation to reach everybody in every time and in every place. He therefore made it very simple. Even a child can read it and get the message. One of the results of this is the ease with which it can be translated.

The verbs are also very simple. One of the verbs used is especially important to our understanding of what took place. Genesis 1 distinguishes between the words 'created' and 'made'. The Hebrew word for 'created', *bara*, means to make something out of nothing and it only occurs three times in the whole of Genesis 1 – to describe the creation of matter, life and man. On other occasions the word 'made' is used instead, to indicate that something is made out of something else, rather in the way we may speak of manufacturing things.

The description of God's work of creation in seven days is also very simple. Each sentence has a subject, a verb and an object. The grammar is so straightforward that anybody can follow it. All the sentences are linked by one word – for example 'but', 'and' or 'then'. It is a remarkable production.

STRUCTURE

Genesis 1 is beautifully structured. It is orderly, spread over six days, and the six days are divided into two sets of three.

In Genesis 1:2 we read, 'Now the earth was formless and empty.' The development starts in verse 3 and there is an amazing correspondence between the first three days and the last three days. In the first three days, God creates a varied environment with sharp contrasts: light from darkness, sky from ocean, and land from sea. He is creating distinctions which make for variety. On the third day he also starts to fill the land with plants. The earth now has 'form'.

Then, on the fourth, fifth and sixth days, he sets out to fill the environments he has created in the first three days. So on day four the sun, moon and stars correspond to the light and darkness created on day one; on day five the birds and fish fill the sky and sea created in day two; and on day six animals and Adam are created to occupy the land created on day three. So God is creating things in an orderly and precise manner. He is indeed bringing order out of chaos. The earth is now 'full' – of life.

MATHEMATICAL PROPERTIES

It also fascinating to note that Genesis 1 has mathematical properties. The three figures that keep coming up in the account are 3, 7 and 10, each of which has particular significance throughout the Bible. The number 3 speaks of what God is, 7 is the perfect number in Scripture, and 10 is the number of completeness. If the occasions when the numbers 3, 7, and 10 occur are examined, some astonishing links emerge.

At only three points does God actually *create* something out of nothing. On three occasions he *calls* something by name, three times he *makes* something, and three times he *blesses* something.

On seven occasions we read that God 'saw that it was good'. There are, of course, seven days – and the first sentence is seven words in Hebrew. Furthermore, the last three sentences in this account of creation are also each formed of seven words in the original Hebrew.

And there are ten commands of God.

SIMPLICITY

The style of Genesis 1 is in marked contrast to other 'creation stories', for example the Babylonian epic of creation, which is very complicated and weird and has little link with reality. The simplicity of the Genesis account of creation has not been universally applauded, however. Some have suggested that this simplistic approach is proof that the Bible cannot be considered as serious in the modern era. But there is much to be said in defence of this simple approach.

Imagine describing how a house is built in a children's book. You would want it to be accurate but simplified so that the young readers would be able to follow the process. You might write about the bricklayer who laid the bricks, the carpenter who worked on the windows, the door frame and the roof joists. You might mention the plumber who put the pipes in, the electrician who came to put the wires in, the plasterer who plasters the walls and the decorator who paints them.

Written in this way the description has six basic stages, but of course building a house is far more complicated than that.

It requires the synchronizing and overlapping of different workers for particular periods of time. No one would say that the description given in the children's book is wrong or misleading, just that it is rather more complex in reality. In the same way there is no doubt that Genesis is a simplification and that science can fill out a whole lot more detail for us. But God's purpose was not to provide detailed scientific accuracy. Rather it was to give an orderly explanation that everyone could follow and accept, and which underlined that he knew what he was doing.

Scientific questions

Understanding the need for simplicity does not answer all the questions which arise from the Genesis account of creation. In particular we must consider the speed at which creation took place and the age of the earth, two separate but interrelated areas. Geologists tell us that the earth must have taken four and a quarter billion years to form, while Genesis seems to say it took just six days. Which is correct?

In terms of the order of creation there is broad agreement between scientists' findings and the Genesis account. Science agrees with the order of Genesis 1, with one exception: the sun, moon and stars do not appear until the fourth day, after the plants are made. This seems contradictory until we realize that the original earth was covered with a thick cloud or mist. Scientific enquiry confirms the likelihood of this. So when the first light appeared, it would just be seen as lighter cloud, whereas once the plants came and started turning carbon dioxide into oxygen, the mist was cleared and for the first time the sun, moon and stars were visible in the sky. The appearance of sun, moon and stars was therefore due to the clearing away of the thick cloud that surrounded the earth. So science does agree exactly with the order of Genesis 1. Creatures appeared in the sea before they appeared on the land. Man appeared last.

While scientists generally agree with the Bible on the order of creation, there are still areas of major conflict. These include the origin of animals and humans and a host of associated questions, including the age of the people who lived before and after the Flood, the extent of the Flood, and the whole question of evolution versus creation.

Before becoming involved in the detail of such questions, however, it is important to note that there are three ways of handling this problem of science versus Scripture. It is vital to decide how you are going to approach the problem before you do so. You must choose whether to repudiate, to segregate or to integrate.

REPUDIATION

The first approach offers a choice. Either Scripture is right, or science is right, but you must repudiate one or the other: you cannot accept both. Typically unbelievers believe science, believers believe Scripture and both bury their heads in the sand about the other.

The problem with repudiating science if you are a Christian is that science has been right in so many areas. We owe so much of our modern communication to scientific development, for example. Science is not the enemy some Christians seem to believe it to be.

The story of the discovery of 'Piltdown man' is a case in point. When a skull from a creature which seemed to be half-man half-ape was discovered at Piltdown in Sussex in 1912, many saw it as evidence of some form of evolution. When it was later found that the skull was actually a forgery, Christians were quick to pour scorn on science. They forgot that it was science which had discovered the skull to be a fake in the first place!

Choosing between science and the Bible thus has problems attached. We should not accept scientific truth unquestioningly, but neither should we be foolish enough to call people to commit intellectual suicide in order to believe the Bible. It is not necessary.

SEGREGATION

The second approach is to keep science and Scripture as far apart as possible. Science is concerned with one kind of truth and Scripture with another. This view claims that science is concerned with physical or material truth, whereas Scripture is concerned with moral and supernatural truth. The two deal with entirely separate issues. Science tells us how and when the world came to be. Scripture tells us who made it and why. They are to be kept entirely separate for there is no overlap to be concerned about. Science talks about facts; Scripture talks about values and we should not look to the one for the other.

This approach has become very common even in churches. It comes from a mindset shaped by Greek thinking, where the physical and the spiritual are kept in two watertight compartments. This kind of thinking is alien to the Hebrew mind, however, which saw God as Creator and Redeemer, with the physical and the spiritual belonging together.

If we take this segregated approach to Genesis we will be forced to treat the narrative as myth. Genesis 3 becomes a fable entitled 'How the snake lost its legs', and Adam becomes 'Everyman'. The book becomes full of fictional stories teaching us values about God and about ourselves, and showing us how to think about God and about ourselves – but we must not press them into historical fact.

Just as Hans Christian Andersen wrote children's books which taught moral values, according to this approach Genesis has stories with moral truths but no historical truth. Adam and Eve were myths, and Noah and the Flood was also a myth. This outlook extends beyond the Genesis narratives, of course, for once one questions the historicity of one section of the Bible it is a small step to question others also. This approach therefore leaves us with no history left in the Bible: plenty of values but few facts.

As with repudiation, then, the attempt to segregate science and Scripture also has its problems. In fact, Scripture and science are like overlapping circles: they do deal with some things that are the same and so apparent contradictions must be faced. And it undermines the whole Bible if we pretend that it is factually inaccurate but still has value. How then are we going to resolve the problem? Can the third approach help us bring science and Scripture together?

INTEGRATION

In trying to understand how to integrate the two, we need to remember two basic things, both equally important: the transitional nature of scientific investigations, and the changes in our interpretation of Scripture.

1. Science changes its views

Scientists used to believe that the atom was the smallest thing in the universe. We know now that each atom is a whole universe in itself. It was said until very recently that the X and Y chromosomes decide whether a foetus becomes a male or a female human being. Now this view has been overturned. The discovery of DNA has revolutionized our thinking about life, because we now know that the earliest form of life had the most complicated DNA. DNA is a language passing on a message from one generation to another – and because of that it must have a person behind it.

A generation ago most people would have understood that nature ran according to fixed laws. Modern science now asserts that there is a much greater randomness than we ever imagined. 'Quantum' physics is much more flexible.

Geology too is changing and developing. There are now many different ways of finding out the age of the earth. Some new methods are claimed to have revealed the age of the earth to be much younger, with 9,000 years at one end of the spectrum and 175,000 years at the other – much less than the four and a quarter billion years calculated previously.

Furthermore, anthropology is in a state of disorder. The prehistoric men thought to be our ancestors are now seen to be creatures which came and disappeared with no link with us. Biology has changed also, and today fewer people believe in the Darwinian concept of evolution.

All this means that while we should not discount the conflicts between scientific discovery and the biblical accounts, we would be foolish to try to tie our interpretation to a particular scientific age, given that scientific knowledge is itself always expanding.

2. Interpretation of Scripture changes

Just as developments occur in scientific understanding, so the traditional interpretations of Scripture can also change. The Bible is inspired by God, but our interpretation of it may not always be. We need to draw a very clear distinction between the Bible text and how we interpret it. When the Bible talks about the four corners of the earth, for example, few people today interpret that to mean the earth is a cube or a square. The Bible uses what is called *the language of appearance*. It talks about the sun rising in the east, setting in the west and running around the sky. But that, as we know, does not mean that the sun is moving around the earth.

Once we understand that scientific interpretation is flexible and that our interpretation of the Bible may change, we can then seek to integrate science and the Bible and make balanced judgements where contradictions seem to exist.

THE 'DAY' IN GENESIS 1

Such an 'integrated' judgement is much needed when we come to consider the arguments regarding the days in Genesis 1, a traditional battlefield in the science versus Scripture debate.

The problem of the days described in Genesis 1 and the real age of the earth was heightened by the fact that some Bibles used to be published with a date alongside the first chapter, namely 4004 BC. This was calculated by an Irish archbishop called James Ussher (another scholar went on to claim that Adam was born at 9 a.m. on 24 October!) All this despite the fact that there are no dates in the original until Chapter 5.

Ussher made his calculations based on the generations recorded in Genesis, unaware that the Jewish genealogies do not include every generation in a line. The words 'son of' may mean grandson or great-grandson. It is easy to discount Ussher's date, but we are still faced with a conflict between the apparent biblical assertion that creation took six days and the scientific assertion that it took much longer.

What was meant by the word 'day' in the original language? This is the Hebrew word *Yom*, which does sometimes mean a day of 24 hours. But it can also mean 12 hours of light or an era of time, as in the phrase 'the day of the horse and cart has gone'.

Bearing these alternative meanings in mind, let us consider the different views of the day in Genesis 1.

Earth days

Some take the word 'day' literally as an earth day of 24 hours. This conflicts with the scientists' assessment of the geological time it would take to create the earth, given its apparent age.

A gap in time

Some suggest a gap in time between verse 2 and verse 3. They argue that after we read that 'the earth was formless' in verse 2, there is a long gap before the six days when God brings everything else into being. So the earth was already in existence before God's work began in the six days. That is a very common theory, found in the Scofield Bible and other Bible notes.

A second way of finding more time is to explain it by reference to the Flood. There have been various books published, notably connected with the names Whitcome and Morris, which have said that the geological data we have all comes out of the Flood, the 'apparent' age of rocks the result of this inundation.

The illusion of time

Others suggest that God deliberately made things look old. Just as Adam was created as a man, not as a baby, so some believe that God made the earth to look older than it really is. God creates genuine antiques! He can make a tree look 200 years old with all the rings in it, and he can create a mountain that looks thousands of years old. It is a possible theory – God could do that.

The 'gap' and 'illusion' views both assume that we take the 'day' literally and therefore need to find more time to make sense of the geological record.

Geological eras

Another approach is to take a 'day' as meaning a 'geological era'. In this case we are not talking about six days, but about six geological ages, i.e. days 1–3 are not solar days (in any case there was no sun!). This is seen as an attractive theory by many, but it fails to account for the morning and evening refrain which is present from day 1, or for the fact that the six days do not correspond to geological ages.

Mythical days

We have already seen that some interpreters have no problem with the length of the days because they assume that the text is mythological anyway. For them the six days are only the poetic framework for the story – fabled days – and can be overlooked. The main thing is to get the moral out of the story and forget the rest.

School days

One of the most intriguing approaches has been put forward by Professor Wiseman of London University. He believes the days were 'educational' days. God revealed his creation in stages to Moses over a seven-day period, so the record we have is of Moses learning about the creative process in the course of a week's schooling. Others agree but suggest that the revelations took the form of visions, rather like the way John was given visions to record for the book of Revelation.

God days

The final possible interpretation is that these were 'God days'. Time is relative to God and a thousand days are like a day to him. It could be understood from this that God was saying that the whole of creation was 'all in a week's work' for him.

This serves to emphasize the importance God attaches to mankind in the scheme of creation, since human life can lose all significance if you take geological time as the only measure. For example, imagine that the height of Cleopatra's Needle on the Thames Embankment in London represents the age of the planet. Place a 10 pence piece flat on top of the needle and a postage stamp on top of that. The 10 pence piece represents the age of the human race and the postage stamp civilized man. Man is seemingly insignificant from a chronological perspective.

Maybe God wanted us to think of creation as a week's work because he wanted to get down to the important part, us living on planet earth. Out of all creation it is we who are most significant to him. He spends such little space in Genesis detailing creation and so much on mankind.

This theory can be extended. The seventh day has no end in the text, because it has lasted centuries. It lasted all the way through the Bible until Easter Sunday, when God raised his son from the dead. All through the Old Testament there is nothing new created; God had finished creation. Indeed, the word 'new' hardly occurs in the Old Testament, and even then is in the negative, as when in Ecclesiastes we read, 'there is nothing new under the sun'. So God rested all the way through the Old Testament.

There is, therefore, a strong argument for seeing the days in Genesis 1 as God days – God himself wanted us to think of it as a week's work.

Man at the centre

Turning to Chapter 2, it is immediately obvious that there is a great difference between this and Chapter 1. There is a shift in style, content and viewpoint. In Chapter 1 God is at the centre and the account of creation is given from his point of view. In Chapter 2 man is given the prominent role. The generic terms of the first chapter give way to specific names in Chapter 2. In Chapter 1 the human race was simply referred to as 'male' and 'female'. In Chapter 2 male and female have become 'Adam' and 'Eve', two particular individuals.

God is also given a name in Chapter 2. In Chapter 1 he was simply 'God' (*Elohim*), but now he is 'the LORD God' (as translated in English Bibles). When we read 'the LORD' in capital letters in our English Bibles it means that in the Hebrew his name is there also. There are no vowels in Hebrew, so his name is made up of four consonants, J H V H, from which the word 'Jehovah' has been coined. This is actually a mistake, because J is pronounced like a Y and V is pronounced like a W. In English pronunciation the letters would therefore be Y H W H, from which we get the word 'Yahweh'. In the New Jerusalem Bible that word is included just as it is – 'The Yahweh God'. We saw earlier how the English word 'always' conveys the meaning of the Hebrew (the participle of the verb 'to be') and it is a helpful word to bring to mind when thinking of God.

Chapter 2 explains more of the relationship between man and God. Chapter 1 included the reference to male and female being made in his image, but in Chapter 2 we see God interacting with man in a way which is unique among all the creatures he had made. There is an affinity between human beings and God that is lacking in every other part of his creation. Animals do not have the ability to have a spiritual relationship with God as humans do. In that sense, humans are like their creator in a unique way.

But we are also told of the differences between God and man, for although man is made in God's image, he is also *unlike* him. This is an important truth to grasp if we are to have a relationship with God. The fact that he is like us means that our relationship with him can be intimate, but the fact that he is unlike us will keep the relationship reverent and ensure that our worship is appropriate. It is possible to be too familiar with God on the one hand, or overawed by him on the other.

The importance of names

The name God gave to Adam meant 'of the earth' – we might call him Dusty. Later in the chapter the woman too is given a name: Eve, meaning 'lively'.

It was normal for names to be descriptive, or even ono-matopoeic (like 'cuckoo'), so when Adam names the animals he uses descriptions which then become their name. Names in the Bible are not only descriptive, they also carry *authority* in them. The person who gives the name has authority over whoever or whatever receives the name. Thus Adam names all the animals, signifying his authority over them. He also names his wife, a feature still remembered today when the woman takes the man's surname when they marry.

This chapter also includes names of places. The land is no longer merely 'dry land': we are told of the land of Havilah, Kush, Asshur and the Garden of Eden. The water is named too. There are four rivers mentioned, and the Tigris and Euphrates are still known today. This puts the Garden of Eden somewhere near north-eastern Turkey, or Armenia, where Mount Ararat stands and where some believe Noah's ark is buried.

Human relationships

In Genesis 2 we see man at the centre of a network of relation-ships. These define the meaning of life. The relationships have three dimensions: to that which is below us, to that which is above us, and to that which is alongside us. Or, to put it another way, we have a vertical relationship to nature below, a vertical relationship to God above, and a horizontal relation-ship with other people and ourselves. Let us look more closely at these three dimensions.

Our relationship to nature. The first dimension is the relationship we have to the other creatures God has made. This relationship is one of subjugation – animals are given to serve mankind. This does not mean we have a licence to be cruel or to make them extinct, but it does mean that animals are further down the scale of value than human beings.

This is an important point to grasp in an age when more value seems to be placed on the protection of baby seals than on preserving the sanctity of the human foetus. Jesus was willing to sacrifice 2,000 pigs in order to save one man's sanity and restore him to his family. In Genesis 9 we read that animals were given to provide food for mankind after the Flood. In relation to nature below us, therefore, we are to have dominion, to cultivate it and control it.

It is interesting to note also in this context that human beings need an environment that is both utilitarian and aesthetic, both useful and beautiful. God did not put man in the wilderness, but planted a garden for him, just as old cottage gardens in England were a mixture of pansies and potatoes – the useful and the beautiful alongside each other.

Our relationship to God. The second dimension is the relationship we have to God above. The nature of this relationship is partly seen in God's command to man concerning two trees in the Garden of Eden: the tree of the knowledge of good and evil and the tree of life. One made life longer and one made life shorter. These trees are not magical trees, but they are what we might call 'sacramental' trees. In the Bible God appoints physical channels to communicate spiritual blessings or curses to us. So eating bread and wine at communion is for our blessing, but eating bread and drinking wine incorrectly or to excess can lead us to be sick or even die. God has appointed physical channels of both grace and judgement. The tree of life tells us that Adam and Eve were not *by nature* immortal, but were *capable* of being immortal. They would not have lived forever by some inherent quality of their own, but only by having access to the tree of life.

No scientist has yet discovered why we die. They have discovered many causes of death, but no one knows why the clock inside us starts winding down. After all, the body is a wonderful machine. If it is supplied with food, fresh air and exercise it could theoretically continue to renew itself. But it does not and no one knows why. The secret is in the tree of life: God was making it possible for human beings to go on living forever by putting that tree in the garden for them. Man was not inherently immortal, but was given the opportunity to attain immortality by feeding on God's constant supply of life.

The tree of knowledge of good and evil is very significant in relation to this. When we read the word 'knowledge', we need to substitute the word 'experience'. The concept of knowledge in the Bible is really 'personal experience'. This idea is present in older versions of the Bible which say, 'Adam *knew* Eve and she conceived and bore a son'. 'Knowledge' in this sense is a personal experience of someone or something. God's command not to touch this tree was given because he did not want them to know (experience) good and evil – he wanted them to retain their innocence. It is similar even today. Once we do a wrong thing we can never be the same as we were. We may be forgiven, but we have lost our innocence.

Why, then, did God put such a tree within their reach? It was his way of saying that he retained moral authority over them. They were not to decide for themselves what was right and wrong, but had to trust God to tell them. Furthermore, he was underlining the fact that they were not landlords on earth, but tenants. The landlord retains the right to set the rules.

The passage also underscores the importance of horizontal relationships, which we shall examine more closely below. Man not only needs to relate to those beneath him and God above him, but also to those alongside him. We are not fully human if we just relate to God and not to other people. We need a network. This understanding is reflected by the Hebrew word *Shalom*, which means 'harmony' – harmony with yourself, with God, with other people and with nature.

In Genesis 2 we have a picture of that harmony and God warns Adam that if he breaks this harmony he will have to die. This will not necessarily be with immediate effect, but his personal 'clock' will begin to wind down.

Some have questioned the severity of the penalty. Death seems a harsh punishment for one little sin. But God was saying that once man had experienced evil, he would have to limit the length of his life on earth, otherwise evil would become eternal. If God allowed rebellious people to live forever they would ruin his universe forever, so he put a time limit on those who would not accept his moral authority.

Our relationship to each other. Man needed a suitable companion. However valuable and valued a pet is, it cannot ever replace personal friendship with another human being. God therefore made Eve to be Adam's companion. We are told in Genesis 1 that male and female are equal in dignity – and we shall see later that they are equal in depravity and in destiny too.

In Genesis 2 we learn that the functions of men and women are different. The Bible talks of the responsibilities of the man to provide and protect, and of the woman to assist and accept. There are three points to note in particular, which are all picked up in the New Testament.

1. **Woman is made from man.** She therefore derives her being from him. Indeed, as we have already seen, woman is named by man just as he named the animals.
2. **Woman is made after man.** He therefore carries the responsibility of the first-born. The significance of that will become clear in Genesis 3, where Adam is blamed for the sin not Eve, since he was responsible for her.
3. **Woman is made for man.** Adam had a job before he had a wife and man is made primarily for his work, while woman is made primarily for relationships. This does not mean that a man must not have relationships or that a woman must not go out to work, but rather that this is the primary purpose for which God made male and female. The fact that man named woman also shows how the partnership is to work: not as a democracy, but with the responsibility of leadership falling to the male. The emphasis is upon co-operation, not competition.

Genesis 2 also deals with other areas fundamental to human relationships. It is clear that sex is good – it is not spelt S-I-N. It is beautiful, indeed God said it was 'very good'. Sex was created for partnership rather than parenthood (an important point which has a bearing on the use of contraception, which plans parenthood without proscribing partnership in intercourse.). Two verses, one in Chapter 1 and one in Chapter 2, are in poetry and both are about sex. God becomes poetic when he considers male and female created in his own image. Then Adam becomes poetic when he catches sight of this beautiful naked girl when he wakes up from the first surgery under anaesthetic. Our English translations of the Hebrew miss the impact. Adam literally exclaims, 'Wow! This is it!' Both little poems convey the delight of God and man in sexuality.

It is clear too that the pattern for sexual enjoyment is monogamy. Marriage is made up of two things, leaving and cleaving, so there is both a physical and a social aspect which together cement the union. One without the other is not a marriage. Sexual intercourse without social recognition is not marriage – it is fornication. Social recognition without consummation is not a marriage either and therefore should be annulled.

We are told that marriage takes precedence over all other relationships. There would be no jokes about parents-in-law if this had been observed throughout history! A person's partner is their first priority before all other relationships, even before their children. Husband and wife are to put each other as absolutely top priority. The ideal painted here in Genesis 2 is of a couple with nothing to hide from each other, with no embarrassment and a total openness to each other. This is an amazing picture and one to which Jesus points centuries later.

Genesis 2 depicts the harmony that should exist in the three levels of relationship between human beings and the created world, God above and our fellow humans. There are, however, some scientific problems to do with the origin of man which must be considered.

Where do prehistoric men fit in?

Evolutionary theory has developed the argument that human beings are descended from the apes. Geological finds suggest that there were prehistoric men who seem to be related to the modern *homo sapiens*. Various remains have been found, specially by the Leakeys, both father and son, in the Orduvi Gorge in Kenya among other places. It is claimed that human life began in Africa, rather than in the Middle East where the Bible puts it.

What are we to make of this evidence? How are we to understand the relationship of modern man to prehistoric man? Is it possible to reconcile what Scripture and science say about the origin of man?

THE ORIGIN OF MAN

Let us look first at what the Bible says. Genesis tells us that man is made of the same material as the animals. The animals were made of the dust of the earth. We too are made of exactly the same minerals that are found in the crust of the earth. A recent estimate indicates that the minerals in a body are worth about 85p! In contrast to the animal world, however, Genesis 2 also tells us that God breathed into the dust and man became a 'living soul'.

Soul

'Soul' is a misunderstood word. The exact phrase is also used of the animals in Genesis 1. They are called 'living souls' because in Hebrew the word 'soul' simply means a breathing body. Since animals and men are both described as 'living souls' they are both the same kind of beings. When we are in danger at sea we send out an SOS not an SOB – but what we want is for our breathing bodies to be saved.

Lord Soper was at Speaker's Corner in Hyde Park one day when he was asked, 'Where is the soul in the body?' He replied, 'Where the music is in the organ!' You can take an organ or a piano to pieces and you will not find the music. It is only there when it is made into a living thing by somebody else.

A special creation

The word 'soul' in Genesis 2 has misled many people into thinking that what makes human beings unique is that we have souls. In fact, we are unique for a different reason. To believe that man and the anthropoid apes came from common stock seems to be in direct opposition to the biblical account. Man is without doubt a special creation. He is made in the image of God, direct from dust and not indirectly from another animal. The Hebrew word *bara*, to create something completely new, is used only three times – of matter, life and man. This implies that there is something unique about man.

The Genesis account emphasizes the unity of the human race too. The apostle Paul told the Athenians that God made us of 'one blood'. Everything in history points to the unity of our human race in the present. I have studied agricultural archaeology a little and it is interesting to note that agricultural archaeology puts the origins of growing corn and domesticating animals exactly where the Bible puts the Garden of Eden, in north-east Turkey or southern Armenia.

SCIENTIFIC SPECULATION

What does science have to say on the matter? Many people would have us choose to accept one side and reject the other: either science has made false investigations into prehistoric man, or Scripture has given us false information.

There is no doubt that science has discovered remains that do look astonishingly like us. They have been given various names: Neanderthal Man, Peking Man, Java Man, Australian Man. The Leakeys claim to have found human remains which date back 4 million years. Among anthropologists it is almost wholly accepted that human origins are to be found in Africa, rather than in the Middle East.

Homo sapiens is said to go back 30,000 years; Neanderthal Man 40–150,000 years; Swanscombe Man 200,000 years; *Homo erectus* (China and Java Man) 300,000 years; Australian Man 500,000 years; and now African Man 4 million years. What are we to say about all this?

The first point which should be made very strongly is that nothing has yet been found that is half-ape and half-man.

There are prehistoric *human* remains, but there is nothing *half-and-half* as yet.

The second point to note is that not all these groups are our direct ancestors. This is now acknowledged by scientists – anthropology is in a state of flux today.

The third point of importance is that the remains do not follow a progressive order. Charts have been produced supposedly showing the development of mankind, starting with the ape on the left-hand side of the chart and moving through successive species to the modern human being, *homo sapiens*, on the right. But these charts are inaccurate: some of the earliest human remains have larger brains than we do today and walked more upright than some of the later remains. The consensus of opinion now is that none of these groups is connected to ours.

There are three possible ways of resolving the conflict. Here they are in very brief outline.

1. **Prehistoric man was biblical man.** What we are digging up was the same as Adam, made in the image of God. It has even been suggested that Genesis 1 portrays 'palaeolithic hunting man', and Genesis 2 portrays 'neolithic farming man'.

2. **Prehistoric man at some point changed into biblical man.** At some point in history this animal-like man or man-like animal became the image of God. Whether just one changed, or a few, or all of them changed at once is open to discussion.

3. **Prehistoric man was not biblical man.** Prehistoric man had a similar physical appearance and used tools, but there is no apparent trace of religion or prayer. He was a different creature, not made in the image of God.

It is unlikely that we need to plump for one explanation over another at this stage. Anthropology is itself in a state of change and development at present, and it is quite likely that the debate will raise other approaches in the future. It is sufficient for us to note the arguments and be aware that any conclusions we draw may well be provisional.

Evolution

Let us turn next to the question of evolution in general. Most people assume that evolution is Charles Darwin's theory. It is not. It was first conceived by Aristotle (384–322 BC). In modern days it was Erasmus Darwin, Charles' grandfather, who first propounded it. Charles picked it up from his atheist grandfather and made it popular.

If we are to grasp the basics of the theory, there are certain terms we need to know.

Variation is the belief that there have been small, gradual changes in form which are passed on to each successive generation. Each generation changes slightly and passes on that change.

From those variations there has been a **natural selection**. This simply means the survival of those most suited to their environment. Take the case of the speckled moth, for example. Against the coal heaps in north-east England the black moth was more suited in camouflage than the white. The birds were able to consume the white moths more easily and the black moths survived. Now that the slag heaps have gone in the area, the white moths are coming back again and the black moths are disappearing. Natural selection is the process whereby those species most adapted to their environment survive. This selection is 'natural' because it happens automatically within nature, with no help from outside.

The belief that there is only a slow, gradual process of variation and selection has now changed, however. A Frenchman called Lamarque said that instead of gradual changes there were sudden, large changes, known as **mutations**. In this situation, progression looks more like a staircase than an escalator.

The concept of **micro-evolution** is that there has been limited change within certain animal groups, e.g. the horse or dog group. Science has certainly proved that micro-evolution does take place.

Macro-evolution, by contrast, is the theory that all animals came from the same origin and that all are related. They all go back to the same simple form of life. This is not change within individual species, therefore, but a belief that all species developed from one another.

The final term to consider is **struggle**. In the context of evolution it refers to the 'survival of the fittest'.

I am not going to argue the case for or against evolution, except to point out that evolution is still a theory. It has not been proven and, in fact, the more evidence we get from fossils the less it looks like being an adequate theory to account for the different forms of life which arose.

1. In the fossil evidence, groups classified separately under evolutionary theory actually appear simultaneously in the Cambrian period. They do not appear gradually over different ages, they appear almost together.

2. Complex and simple forms of life appear together. There is not a sequence from the simple to the complex.

3. There are very, very few 'bridge' fossils that are halfway between one species and another.

4. All life forms are very complicated: they have always had DNA.

5. Mutations, the sudden changes which are purported to account for the development from one species to the next, usually lead to deformities and cause creatures to die out.

6. Interbreeding usually leads to sterility.
7. Above all, when the statistical probabilities are analysed, quite apart from the other objections, there is not enough time for all the varieties of life form to have developed.

The theory of evolution is not merely of academic interest, of course. How we each understand our origins has an effect on how we view mankind as a whole. Leaders infected by evolutionist philosophy have had a considerable impact.

Basic to the evolutionist theory is the concept of the survival of the fittest and the struggle which all species face to survive. This is found in some of the philosophies which have shaped our civilized society, and it has caused untold suffering. American capitalists such as John D. Rockefeller have said, 'Business is the survival of the fittest.' A similar outlook is found in fascism: Adolf Hitler's book was called *Mein Kampf*, 'My Struggle'. He believed in the survival of the fittest, the 'fittest' being in his view the German Aryan race. It is also found in communism. Karl Marx wrote about the 'struggle' between the bourgeoisie and the proletariat, which he believed must issue in revolution. The word 'struggle' could also be written across the early days of colonialism, when people were simply wiped out in the name of progress.

In short, the idea of the survival of the fittest when applied to human beings has caused more suffering than any other concept in modern times. But it has also faced us with two huge choices as to what we believe.

MENTAL CHOICE

It faces us first with a mental choice. If you believe in creation you believe in a father God. If you believe in evolution you tend to go for mother nature (a lady who does not exist). If you believe in creation you believe that this universe was the result of a personal choice. If you believe in evolution, you will argue that it was a random, impersonal chance. There was a designed purpose under creation, but under evolution only a random pattern. With creation the universe is a supernatural production, in evolution it is a natural process. Under creation the whole universe is an open situation, open to personal intervention by both God and man. In evolution we have nature as a closed system that operates itself. In creation we have the concept of providence, that God cares for his creation and provides for it and looks after it. But with evolution we simply have coincidence: if anything good happens it is merely the result of chance. With creation we have a faith based on fact, with evolution a faith based on fancy (for it is just a theory). If we accept creation then we accept that God is free to make something and to make man in his image. If we accept evolution we are left with the view that man is free to make God in whatever image he chooses out of his imagination. Accepting one or the other, therefore, has considerable ramifications.

MORAL CHOICE

There is also a moral choice behind accepting creation or evolution. Why is it that people seize on the theory of evolution and hold onto it so fanatically? The answer is that it is the only real alternative if you want to believe that there is no God over us. Under creation *God* is Lord, under evolution *man* is Lord. With creation we are under divine authority, but if there is no God we are autonomous as humans and can decide things for ourselves. If we accept God as creator we accept that there are absolute standards of right and wrong. But with no God under evolution, we only have relative situations. With God's world we talk of duty and responsibility, with evolution we talk of demands and rights. Under God we have an infinite dependence, we become as little children and speak to the heavenly father. With evolution we are proud of our independence, we speak of coming of age, of no longer 'needing' God. According to the Bible, man is a fallen creature. According to evolution he is rising and progressing all the time. In the Bible we have salvation for the weak. In evolutionary philosophy we have the survival of the strong.

Nietzsche, the philosopher behind the thought in Hitler's Germany, said he hated Christianity because it kept weak people going and looked after the sick and dying. The Bible teaches that you are powerful when you do what is right, but evolutionary philosophy leads to a 'might is right' outlook. One leads to peace, the other to war. Where evolutionism says you should indulge yourself, look after number one, the Bible says that faith, hope and love are the three main virtues in life. Ultimately the Bible leads us to heaven, whereas evolution promises little – fatalism, helplessness and luck – and leads to hell.

The Fall

When God finished creating our world he said that it was very good. Few today would say that it is a very good world now. Something went wrong. Genesis 3 describes for us what the problem is and how it arose.

There are three undeniable facts about our existence today:

1. Birth is painful.
2. Life is hard.
3. Death is certain.

Why is this? Why is birth painful? Why is life hard? Why is death certain?

Philosophy gives us many different answers. Some philosophers say there must be a bad God as well as a good one. More frequently, they say that the good God made a bad job of it and try to find in that some explanation for the origin of evil. Genesis 3 gives us four vital insights into this problem.

1. Evil was not always in the world.
2. Evil did not start with human beings.
3. Evil is not something physical, it is something moral. Some philosophers have said that it is the material part of the universe that is the source of evil, or in personal terms it is your body that is the source of temptation.
4. Evil is not a thing that exists on its own. It is an adjective rather than a noun. Evil as such does not exist, it is only persons who can be or become evil.

So what does Genesis 3 have to teach us on the subject? It is worth reminding ourselves that this is a real event in real history: we are given both the place and the time of it. At the dawn of human history a gigantic moral catastrophe took place.

The problem starts with a speaking reptile (more a lizard than a snake because it had legs, despite conventional wisdom; it was only later that God made the serpent slither on its belly). How are we to understand this extraordinary story of the snake speaking to Eve? There are three possibilities:

1. The serpent was the devil in disguise; he can appear as an angel or an animal.
2. God enabled an animal to talk, as he did with Balaam's ass.
3. The animal was possessed by an evil spirit. Just as Jesus sent the demons tormenting a man down the Gadarene cliffs into the bodies of 2,000 pigs, so it is perfectly possible for Satan to take over an animal. This would fool Adam and Eve, because Satan was putting himself below them. In fact Satan is a fallen angel, just as real as human beings, more intelligent and stronger than we are.

It is significant that Satan went for Eve. In very general terms, women tend to be more trusting than men, who are notoriously distrustful. Capitalizing on this, Satan subverts God's order and treats Eve as if she were the head of the house. Although it is clear that Adam is there with Eve, he says nothing. He should be protecting her, arguing with Satan. After all, it was Adam who had heard God's words of prohibition.

All told, there are three ways of misquoting the Word of God. One is to add something to it, another is to take something away, and a third is to change what is there. If you read the text carefully, you will find that Satan did all three. Satan knows his Bible very well, but he can misquote it and manipulate it too. Adam, however, who knew exactly what God had said, kept silent when he should have spoken up. In the New Testament he is clearly blamed for allowing sin to enter the world.

It is useful to note the strategy which Satan adopts in his approach to Eve. First he encourages doubt with the mind, second desire with the heart, and third disobedience with the will. This is always his strategy in all his dealings with humans. He encourages wrong thinking first, usually by misinterpreting God's Word. Next he entices us to desire evil in our hearts. After that the circumstances are right for us to disobey with our wills.

What is the outcome of sin? When God questions Adam he seeks to blame both Eve and God. He speaks of 'that woman you gave me', or 'the woman you put here with me'. He ceased to fulfil his role as a man by denying his responsibility to look after his wife.

God responds in judgement. This side of his character is seen for the first time: God hates sin and he must deal with it. If he is really a good God, then he cannot let people get away with badness. This is the message of Genesis 3. The punishment is given in poetic form. When God speaks in prose he is communicating his thoughts, from his mind to your mind, but when he speaks poetically he is communicating his feelings, from his heart to yours.

In Genesis 3 the poems reveal God's angry emotions (the wrath of God, in theological terms). God feels so deeply that Eden has been ruined – and he knows too where this will lead. The following paraphrase of Genesis 1–3 sheds a fresh light on this story.

A long time ago, when nothing else existed, the God who had always been there brought the entire universe into being, the whole of outer space and this planet earth.

At first the earth was just a mass of fluid matter, quite uninhabitable and indeed uninhabited. It was shrouded in darkness and engulfed in water; but God's own spirit was hovering just above the flood.

Then God commanded: 'Let the light in!' And there it was. It looked just right to God, but he decided to alternate light with darkness, giving them different names: 'day' and 'night'. The original darkness and the new light were the evening and the morning of God's first working day.

Then God spoke again: 'Let there be two reservoirs of water, with an expanse between them'. So he separated the water on the surface from the moisture in the atmosphere. That's how the 'sky', as God called it, came to be. This ended his second day's work.

The next thing God said was: 'Let the surface water be concentrated in one area, so that the rest may dry out.' Sure enough, it happened! From then on, God referred to 'sea' and 'land' separately. He liked what he saw and added: 'Now let the land sprout vegetation, plants with seed and trees with fruit, all able to reproduce themselves'. And they appeared –

all kinds of plant and tree, each able to propagate its own type. Everything fitted into God's plan. His third day's work was over.

Now God declared: 'Let different sources of light appear in the sky. They will distinguish days from nights and make it possible to measure seasons, special days and years; though their main purpose will be to provide illumination.' And so it is, just as he said. The two brightest lights are the larger 'sun' that dominates the day and the lesser 'moon' which predominates at night, surrounded by twinkling stars. God put them all there for earth's sake – to light it, regulate it and maintain the alternating pattern of light and darkness. God was pleased that his fourth day's work had turned out so well.

The next order God issued was: 'Let the sea and the sky teem with living creatures, with shoals of swimming fish and flocks of flying birds.' So God brought into being all the animated things that inhabit the oceans, from huge monsters of the deep to the tiny organisms floating in the waves, and all the variety of birds and insects on the wing in the wind above. To God it was a wonderful sight and he encouraged them to breed and increase in numbers, so that every part of sea and sky might swarm with life. That ended his fifth day.

Then God announced: 'Now let the land also teem with living creatures – mammals, reptiles and wildlife of every sort.' As before, no sooner was it said than done! He made all kinds of wildlife, including mammals and reptiles, each as a distinct type. And they all gave him pleasure.

At this point God reached a momentous decision: 'Now let's make some quite different creatures, more our kind – beings, just like us. They can be in charge of all the others – the fish in the sea, the birds of the air and the animals on the land.

To resemble himself God created mankind,
To reflect in themselves his own heart, will and mind,
To relate to each other, male and female entwined.

Then he affirmed their unique position with words of encour-
agement: 'Produce many offspring, for you are to occupy and
control the whole earth. The fish in the sea, the birds of the air
and the animals on the land are all yours to master. I am also
giving you the seed-bearing plants and the fruit-bearing trees
as your food supply. The birds and the beasts can have the
green foliage for their food.' And so it was.

God surveyed all his handiwork and he was very satisfied
with it ... everything so right, so beautiful ... six days' work
well done.

Outer space and planet earth were now complete. Since
nothing more was needed, God took the next day off. That is
why he designated every seventh day to be different from the
others, set apart for himself alone – because on that day he
was not busy with his daily work on creation.

This is how our universe was born and how everything
in it came to be the way it is; when the God whose name is
'Always' was making outer space and the planet earth, there
was a time when there was no vegetation at all on the
ground. And if there had been, there was neither any rain
to irrigate it nor any man to cultivate it. But underground
springs welled up to the surface and watered the soil. And the
God 'Always' moulded a human body from particles of clay,
gave it the kiss of life, and man joined the living creatures.
And the God 'Always' had already laid out a stretch of
parkland, east of here, a place called 'Eden', which means
'Delight'. He brought the first man there to live. The God
'Always' had planted a great variety of trees in the part with
beautiful foliage and delicious fruit. Right in the middle were

two rather special trees; fruit from one of them could maintain life indefinitely while the fruit of the other gave the eater personal experience of doing right and wrong.

One river watered the whole area but divided into four branches as it left the park. One was called the Pishon and wound across the entire length of Havilah, the land where pure nuggets of gold were later found, as well as aromatic resin and onyx. The second was called the Gihon and meandered right through the country of Cush. The third was the present Tigris, which flows in front of the city of Asshur. The fourth was what we know as the Euphrates.

So the God 'Always' set the man in this 'Parkland of Delight' to develop and protect it. And the God 'Always' gave him very clear orders: 'You are perfectly free to eat the fruit of any tree except one – the tree that gives experience of right and wrong. If you taste that you will certainly have to die the death.'

Then the God 'Always' said to himself: 'It isn't right for the man to be all on his own. I will provide a matching partner for him.'

Now the God 'Always' had fashioned all sorts of birds and beasts out of the soil and he brought them in contact with the man to see how he would describe them; and whatever the man said about each one became its name. So it was man who labelled all the other creatures but in none of them did he recognize a suitable companion for himself.

So the God 'Always' sent the man into a deep coma and while he was unconscious God took some tissue from the side of his body, and pulled the flesh together over the gap. From the tissue he produced a female clone and introduced her to the man, who burst out with:

'At last you have granted my wish,
A companion of my bones and flesh,
"Woman" to me is her name,
Wooed by the man whence she came.'

All this explains why a man lets go of his parents and holds on to his wife, their two bodies melting into one again.

The first man and his new wife wandered about the park quite bare, but without the slightest embarrassment.

Now there was a deadly reptile around, more cunning than any of the wild beasts the God 'Always' had made. He chatted with the woman one day and asked: 'You don't mean to tell me that God has actually forbidden you to eat any fruit from all these trees?' She replied: 'No, it's not quite like that. We can eat fruit from the trees, but God did forbid us to eat from that one in the middle. In fact, he warned us that if we even touch it, we'll have to be put to death.'

'Surely he wouldn't do that to you,' said the reptile to the woman, 'he's just trying to frighten you off because he knows perfectly well that when you eat that fruit you'd see things quite differently. Actually it would put you on the same level as him, able to decide for yourself what is right and wrong.'

So she took a good look at the tree and noticed how nourishing and tasty the fruit appeared to be. Besides, it was obviously an advantage to be able to make one's own moral judgements. So she picked some, ate part and gave the rest to her husband, who was with her at the time and he promptly ate too. Sure enough, they did see things quite differently! For the first time they felt self-conscious about their nudity. So they tried to cover up with crude clothes stitched together from fig leaves.

That very evening, they suddenly became aware of the approach of the God 'Always' and ran to hide in the undergrowth. But the God 'Always' called out to the man: 'What have you got yourself into?' He answered: 'I heard you coming and I was frightened because I haven't got any decent clothes. So I'm hiding in the bushes over here.' Then God demanded: 'How did you discover what it feels like to be naked? Have you been eating the fruit I ordered you to leave alone?' The man tried to defend himself: 'It's all due to that woman you sent along; she brought this fruit to me, so naturally I just ate it without question.'

Then the God 'Always' challenged the woman: 'What have you been up to?' The woman said: 'It's that dreadful reptile's fault! He deliberately deluded me and I fell for it.'

So the God 'Always' said to the reptile: 'As a punishment for your part in this:

> Above all the beasts I will curse
> Your ways with a fate that is worse!
> On your belly you'll slither and thrust
> With your mouth hanging down in the dust.
> For the rest of the days in your life,
> There'll be terror, hostility, strife
> Between woman and you for this deed
> Which you'll both pass along to your seed;
> But his foot on your skull you will feel
> As you strike out in fear at his heel.'

Then to the woman he said:

> 'Let the pain of child-bearing increase
> The agony, labour and stress;
> You'll desire a man to control
> But find yourself under his rule.'

But to the man, Adam, he said, 'Because you paid attention to your wife rather than me and disobeyed my order prohibiting that tree:

> There's a curse on the soil;
> All your days you will toil.
> Thorns and thistles will grow
> Among all that you sow.
> With a brow running sweat
> You will labour to eat;
> Then return to the ground
> In the state you were found.
> From the clay you were made;
> In the dust you'll be laid.'

Adam gave his wife the name Eve (it means 'life-giving') because he now realized she would be the mother of all human beings who would ever live.

The God 'Always' made some new clothes from animal skins for Adam and his wife and got them properly dressed. Then the God 'Always' said to himself; 'Now this man has become as conscious of good and evil things as we have been, how could we limit the damage if he is still able to eat from the other special tree and live as long as us?' To prevent this happening, the God 'Always' banished the man from the Park of Delight and sent him back to cultivate the very same patch of ground from which he was originally moulded!

After he had been expelled, heavenly angels were stationed on the eastern border of the Park of Delight, guarding access to the tree of continuous life with sharp, scorching weapons.

THE RESULTS OF THE FALL

Chapter 3 is usually referred to as 'the Fall', when man fell from the beautiful state described in Chapter 2. It could all have been so different. If Adam had not tried to blame Eve, or even God, but had responded in repentance, God could have forgiven him on the spot. History might have been very different. Instead we have Adam's pathetic attempt at cover-up with fig leaves to mirror his folly.

The nature of the punishment is well worthy of note. Adam is punished in relation to his work, and Eve in relation to the family. The reptile becomes a snake (even today there are very small legs on the underside of a snake).

Their former relationship with God is destroyed. Their relationship with each other is also affected: they hide from each other and God pronounces a curse over them. In Chapter 4 the first murder takes place within the family, as envy gives way to defiance against God's warning.

Let us now focus on three areas in the subsequent story where God's reactions to the situation are especially seen.

1. Cain

Somebody has pointed out that the sin committed by the first man caused the second man to kill the third. Here we have Adam's own family. His eldest son kills his middle son, and for the same reason that they killed Jesus centuries later: envy. Envy was responsible for the first murder in history and the worst murder in history.

Cain means 'gotten' – when he was born, Eve said 'I have gotten' (in the King James translation) him from the Lord. Abel means 'breath' or 'vapour'. God favoured Abel, the younger child of the two, because he did not want anybody ever to think they had a natural right to his gifts and inheritance. Often in Scripture we see God choose a younger person over an older one (e.g. Isaac over Ishmael, Jacob over Esau).

The problem that divided them was that God accepted Abel's sacrifice and rejected Cain's. Abel had learned from his parents that the only sacrifice worthy of God was a blood sacrifice – the result of a life being taken. God had already covered the sin and shame of his parents by killing animals and providing a covering for Adam and Eve from their skins. A principle was being established: blood was shed so that their shame could be covered (it began there and continues through to Calvary). So when Abel came to worship God he brought an animal sacrifice. Cain simply brought fruit and vegetables.

God was only pleased with Abel's sacrifice, not with Cain's offering. Cain was angered by this. In spite of God's warning that he should master sin, Cain leads his brother away from his home on a false pretext, then murders him, buries him and totally disowns him ('Am I my brother's keeper?' he asks).

A clear pattern emerges here: bad people hate good people, and the ungodly are envious of the godly. This is a division that goes all the way through human history.

So God's perfect world is now a place where goodness is hated, and the evil people excuse their wickedness. Anyone who presents a challenge to the conscience is hated. We could say that Abel was the first martyr for righteousness' sake. Jesus himself said that the 'blood of the righteous has been spilled from Abel, right through to Zechariah'.

The narrative goes on to chart the line of Cain and it includes some interesting elements. Alongside the names of Cain's descendants are listed their achievements, most notably the development of music and of metallurgy, including the first weapons. Urbanization also came from Cain's line. It was Cain's line that began to build cities, concentrating sinners in one place and therefore concentrating sin in one place. It could be said that cities became more sinful than the countryside because of this concentration.

Thus what we might see as 'human progress' is tainted. The 'mark of Cain', as it were, is on these 'developments', and that is the biblical interpretation of civilization: sinful activity is always at its heart. Polygamy also came through Cain's line. Up to that point one man and one woman were married for life, but Cain's descendants took many wives, and we know that even Abraham, Jacob and David were polygamists.

There was a third brother, however, Adam and Eve's third son Seth. With him we see another line beginning, a Godly line. From the line of Seth, men began to 'call on the name of the LORD'.

These two lines run right through human history and will continue to do so right to the end, when they will be separated for ever. We live in a world in which there is a line of Cain and a line of Seth, and we can choose which line we belong to and which kind of life we wish to live.

2. Noah

The next major event is the Flood and the building of Noah's ark. The story is well known, both inside and outside the Bible. Many peoples have tales of a universal flood within their folklore. It has been questioned whether it was a real event and whether it literally covered the whole earth. The text does not indicate whether the Flood went right round the globe or just covered the then known world. Certainly the Middle Eastern basin, later called Mesopotamia, the huge plain through which the Tigris and the Euphrates flow, is the scene of all the early stories of Genesis and was definitely an area affected by flood.

The Bible's focus is not so much on the material side of this story as on the moral side. Why did it happen? The answer is staggering. It happened because God regretted that he had made human beings. 'His heart was filled with pain'. This is surely one of the saddest verses in the Bible. It communicates God's feelings so clearly, and these led to his resolve to wipe out the human race.

What had happened to cause such a crisis in God's emotions? To answer this we need to piece together the Genesis narrative with some parts of the New Testament and some extra-testamental material quoted in Jude and Peter.

We are told that between two and three hundred angels in the area of Mount Hermon sent to look after God's people fell in love with women, seducing them and impregnating them. The offspring were a horrible hybrid, somewhere between men and angels – beings not in God's order. These are the 'Nephilim' in Genesis 6 – the offspring of the union between the 'sons of God' and the 'daughters of men'. The word is sometimes translated as 'giants' in English versions. We do not know exactly what is meant – it is just a new term for a new sort of creature. This horrible combination was also the beginning of occultism, because those angels taught the women witchcraft. There are no traces of occult practices before this event.

The immediate effect of this perverted sex was that violence filled the whole earth; the one leads to the other when people are treated as objects and not as persons. Genesis 6 tells us that God saw that 'every imagination of man's heart was only evil continually'. He felt that enough was enough.

But God did not judge immediately, he was very patient and gave them full warning. He called Enoch to be a prophet to tell the human race that God was coming to judge and deal with all ungodliness. At the age of 65 Enoch had a son, and God gave him the name for the boy, Methuselah, which means 'When he dies it will happen'. So both Methuselah and Enoch knew that when Enoch's son died God would judge the world.

We know that God was patient, because Methuselah lived longer than anybody else who has ever lived – 969 years. When Methuselah died it began to rain heavily. Methuselah's grandson was called Noah. He and his three sons had spent 12 months building a huge covered raft according to God's specifications. Just one family, a preacher and his three boys, three daughters-in-law and his wife, were saved.

After the Flood, God promised never to repeat such a thing as long as the earth remained. He made a covenant, a sacred promise with the whole human race: not only would he never destroy the human race again, but he would support them by providing enough food. He would ensure that summer, winter, springtime and harvest came regularly. At a time when famine is common in various parts of the world, this promise may seem to have been ignored. But there is far more corn in the world than we need – it is just not evenly distributed. Everyone could be fed if the political will existed.

God put a rainbow in the sky to signify this covenant. The two things we need for life on earth are sunlight and water, and when they come together the rainbow is visible.

When God made this promise he also demanded something of mankind. He commanded that we must treat human life as sacred and therefore punish murder with execution. When a nation abolishes capital punishment, it says something about its view of human life.

3. Babel

The next incident that affected God deeply was the building of the Tower of Babel. People wanted to build a tower that reached into God's sphere of heaven, effectively to 'challenge heaven'. The text says that they wanted to build a name for themselves. We know roughly what the tower would have looked like: such a tower was called a *ziggurat*, a great brick structure with staircases extending heavenwards. On the top of such towers there were usually astrological signs. But it was not so much for worshipping stars that Nimrod (king of Babylon, or Babel) built that tower – it was more to express his own power and grandeur.

The Tower of Babel offended God very profoundly. He said that if he let them continue there was no telling where it would end. So God gave the gift of tongues for the first time, to confuse the people. They could no longer understand each other. From then on humanity split, scattering and speaking different languages.

There is an interesting footnote to the story of Babel. Among the people scattered at Babel were a group who climbed over the mountains to the east and eventually settled when they reached the sea. They became the great nation of China. Chinese culture goes right back to that day. They left the area of Babel before the Cuneiform alphabet replaced the picture language of ancient Egypt. All languages were pictorial right up to the time of Babel. The language they took to China they put down in picture form. The amazing thing is that it is possible to reconstruct the story from Genesis 1 to 11 by looking at the symbols which the Chinese use to describe different words.

The Chinese word for 'create', for example, is made up of the pictures for mud, life and someone walking. Their word for 'devil' is made up of a man, a garden, and the picture for secret. So the devil is a secret person in the garden. Their word for 'tempter' is made up of the word for 'devil' plus two trees and the picture for cover. Their word for 'boat' is made up of container, mouth and eight, so a boat in the Chinese language is a vessel for eight people, as was Noah's ark.

We can reconstruct the whole of Genesis 1–11 from the picture language in China. When these people first arrived in

China, therefore, they believed in one God, the maker of heaven and earth. It was only after Confucius and Buddha that they got involved in idolatry. The Chinese language is an independent confirmation from outside the Bible that these things happened and were carried in the memories of people scattered at Babel, who then settled in China.

JUSTICE AND MERCY

Two themes predominate in these chapters: from the Fall of Adam onwards we see both human pride and God's response of justice and mercy. He showed justice to Adam and Eve in banishing them from the garden and telling them that they would one day die, but also mercy in providing a covering for them. He showed justice to Cain in condemning him to be a wanderer, but mercy in placing a mark on him so that no one would kill him. He punished the generation of Enoch (although not Enoch himself), but we see his mercy in saving Noah and his family and his patience in waiting, as he gave Methuselah such a long life. What does the rest of Genesis tell us about God? Let us look further, and see what kind of relationship he had with his people through the generations and events which followed.

The sovereign God

There is a double thread running right through the portrayal of God in the Old Testament which requires an explanation. It is a juxtaposition which only becomes clear through reading the book of Genesis.

The God of the Jews

On the one side the Old Testament claims that the God of the Jews is the God of the whole universe. In those days every nation had its own god, whether it was Baal, or Isis, or Molech, and religion was strictly national. All wars were religious wars, between nations with different gods. Israel's God (Yahweh) was considered by other nations to be just the national god of Israel. But Israel herself claimed that her God was 'the God above all Gods'. Indeed, the Israelites went even further, asserting that their God was the only God who really existed. He had made the entire universe. All the other gods were figments of human imagination. These claims were, of course, extremely offensive to the other nations. You can read of them in Isaiah 40, in the book of Job and in many of the psalms.

The God of the whole universe

The other side of the picture painted in the Old Testament is that the God of the whole universe is the God of the Jews. They were claiming that the creator of everything had a very personal and intimate relationship with them, one little group of people on earth. In fact, they were claiming that he had identified himself with one family; with a grandfather, a father and a son. According to them, the God of the entire universe called himself 'the God of Abraham, Isaac and Jacob'. It was an incredible claim.

God's plan

This astonishing two-fold truth that the God of the Jews is the God of the universe, and the God of the universe is especially the God of the Jews, is explained for us in Genesis – indeed, without this book we would have no ground for believing it.

The book of Genesis covers more time than the whole of the rest of the Bible put together. The beginning of Exodus to the end of Revelation covers around 1,500 years, a millennium and a half, whereas Genesis alone covers the entire history of the world from its beginning right through to the time of

Joseph. So when we read the Bible we must realize that time has been compressed, and that Genesis covers many centuries compared to the rest of the Bible.

This time compression is also true within Genesis itself. We have noted already that Chapters 1–11 form a quarter of the book and yet cover a very long period and a considerable breadth of people and nations. The second 'part' of Genesis, Chapters 12–50, is a much longer section taking up three-quarters of the book, yet it only covers a relatively few years and a few people – just one family and only four generations of that family. This seems to be a huge disproportion of space if Genesis is claiming to tell the history of our whole world.

It is clear, however, that this difference in proportions is quite deliberate. There is a deliberate move away from looking at the whole world to focus in on one particular family as if they were the most important family ever to have lived. In one sense they were, for they were part of that very special line from Seth of people who called on the name of the Lord. As far as God was concerned, the people who called on him were more important than anyone else because they were the people through whom he could fulfil his plans and purposes.

This approach serves to remind us that the Bible is not God's answers to our problems; it is God's answer to God's problem. God's problem was: 'What do you do with a race that doesn't want to know you or love you or obey you?' One solution was to wipe them out and start again. He tried that, but even the father of the righteous remnant saved through the Flood (Noah) got drunk and exposed himself, demonstrating that human nature had not changed. But God did not give up. He was concerned about human beings; he had created them. He had one son already and he enjoyed that son so much he wanted a bigger family, so he was not about to give up on the problem of mankind.

His solution began with Abraham. Philosophers call this 'the scandal of particularity', suggesting that God was being unfair in choosing to deal only with the Jews. Why did he not save the Chinese through the Chinese, the Americans through the Americans, the British through the British? God's rescue programme is an offence to us – summed up by the poet William Norman Ewer:

> How odd
> Of God
> To choose
> The Jews.

Then Cecil Browne decided to add a second verse in reply:

> But not so odd
> As those who choose
> A Jewish God,
> But spurn the Jews.

We might explain God's approach by considering a simple domestic situation. A father decides to bring home sweets for his three children. He could bring three bars of chocolate and give them one each, or he could bring a bag of sweets, give it to one child and tell them to share. The first option is the most peaceful one, but treats the children as unconnected individuals. If he wants to create a *family* then the second approach would teach them more.

God's way, therefore, was to start a plan whereby his son would come as a Jew. He told the Jews to share his blessings with everyone else, instead of dealing with each nation separately. He chose the Jews, with the intention that all other peoples might know his blessing through them.

This is why he calls himself the God of Abraham, Isaac and Jacob in the Old Testament. Chapters 12–50 of Genesis are basically the stories of just four men. Three are classed together while the fourth, Joseph, is treated separately – for reasons which will become apparent later, when we focus on him in some detail.

Built into the stories of the first three men are contrasts with other relatives. The counterpoint to Abraham is his nephew Lot; the counterpoint to Isaac is his stepbrother Ishmael; the counterpoint to Jacob is his twin brother Esau. The relationships become progressively closer, from nephew to stepbrother to twin. God is showing that there are still two lines running through the human race in very stark contrast to each other. The stories invite us to line ourselves up with one side or the other. Are you a Jacob or an Esau? Are you an Isaac or an Ishmael? Are you an Abraham or a Lot?

ARE THESE STORIES REAL?

There are some who argue that these chapters are legends or sagas. They say that while there is a nucleus of truth in them, they cannot be confirmed as historically accurate. What such people forget is that 'fiction' is a very recent form of literature. Novels were totally unknown in Abraham's day. There would have been little point in writing invented stories. Indeed, if you were committed to inventing a story about a hero figure, you would doubtless ascribe miracles to them. The Genesis record includes hardly any at all. There are dozens in the book of Exodus, but Genesis has very few. Yet legend is usually full of miraculous or magical happenings.

Furthermore, nobody has found a single anachronism in these stories (an anachronism being the inclusion of material which could not have taken place in that time period). The cultural details that emerge in these stories have been shown by archaeology to be totally true.

The one feature that cannot be accounted for by natural explanation is the part which angels play, but they are involved throughout the Bible. If you have problems with angels you have problems with the whole Bible. Apart from that, these stories are very ordinary – they are about ordinary men and women who are born, fall in love, marry, have children and die. They keep sheep and goats and cattle and grow a few crops. They disagree, they quarrel, they fight; they erect tents, they build altars and they worship God. All these things are totally within the range of normal human experience.

WHY DID GOD CHOOSE THE JEWS?

What *is* different about these stories, however, is that God talks with the people in them and they talk to him. So we find that the God of the entire universe makes a special friend called Abraham. Indeed, God calls him 'Abraham my friend'. This is the scandal of particularity. People cannot cope with a God who makes personal friends. They feel that somehow it is inappropriate, and yet that is the truth of what happens here.

The big question is: Why should God choose to identify himself as the God of Abraham, Isaac and Jacob? What is so special about them? This has been the question asked by other nations, other peoples, down through the ages. What is so special about the Jews? Why should they be the chosen people and not us?

The answer lies in God's sovereign choice. These three men had no *natural* claim on God. He freely initiated the relationship with them and they could not claim that the relationship was down to them. Indeed, in each of the generations it is striking how the typical rights of inheritance are overturned. The first son would normally inherit the family wealth from the father, but in each generation God chooses not the eldest but the youngest son. He chooses Isaac, not Ishmael, and

Jacob, not Esau. He is thus establishing that no one has a natural claim on his love: it is just his love to give as he chooses. It was not, therefore, a question of a straight hereditary link through the eldest son. Neither Isaac nor Jacob were the firstborn. What they inherited was a free gift.

More striking is the fact that none of these three men had a *moral* claim on God either, for they could not claim to be better than anyone else. In fact, the Bible states how each man lied to get himself out of a tricky situation. Both Abraham and Isaac lied through their teeth about their own wives to save their skins, and Jacob was the worst of the three. Not only were these men liars, they also took more than one wife. We are given a picture of very ordinary men like us who all had their weaknesses.

The only thing they had which did mark them out was *faith*. These men believed in God. God can do wonders when a person believes. God would rather have a believing person than a good person – he even said to Abraham that his faith went down in his book as 'righteousness'. Good deeds without a belief in God count for nothing.

Isaac and Jacob shared that faith, although they were very different in personality and temperament. The one common thing between the three men was that they had faith.

The faith of the patriarchs

Abraham's faith was especially evident when he left Ur of the Chaldees. The city was a very impressive, sophisticated place, one of the most advanced anywhere in the world, but God told Abraham he wanted him to live in a tent for the rest of his life. Not many of us would leave a comfortable city and live in a tent up in the mountains where it is cold and snows in winter, especially at the age of 75. God told him to leave a land he would never see again in order to go to a land he had never seen before. He must leave his family and friends (although in the event Abraham actually took his father and other members of his family halfway as far as Haran, from where he and his nephew Lot continued the journey). Abraham obeyed. He even believed God when he told him he would have a son despite his wife Sarah being 90 years old. (When the boy came they called him 'Joke'. *Isaac* is Hebrew for 'laugh'. When Sarah first heard that she was going to be pregnant at that age she just roared with laughter.)

Abraham's faith had considerable knocks along the way. Eleven years passed after God's promise and there was still no sign of a son. Abraham, at Sarah's suggestion, sought offspring through her maidservant Hagar. The Bible makes it clear that Ishmael was not a 'child of faith', but a 'child of the flesh' whom God did not choose (although God went on to bless him too with many generations of offspring which make up the Arab peoples today).

When Isaac eventually came, Abraham exercised faith when he was prepared to sacrifice him on an altar at God's request. The Bible tells us that Abraham was willing to kill Isaac as a sacrifice because he believed God would raise him from the dead after he had killed him. Considering that God had never done that before, this was some faith. He reasoned that if God could produce life (Isaac) from his old body, he could surely bring Isaac back from the dead if he wanted.

Most of the pictorial representations of the sacrifice of Isaac paint him as a boy of 12. But if we examine the text surrounding this event we see that the very next thing that happens is Sarah's death at the age of 127, which would make Isaac 37. So Isaac was probably in his early thirties at the time of the sacrifice. He could therefore have resisted easily, but he submitted in faith to his father Abraham, an old man. (The location is also significant, for the mountain of sacrifice was called Moriah, which later became Golgotha, or Calvary.) Isaac also demonstrates faith in other ways, principally in trusting Abraham's servant to find him a wife.

Jacob too had faith, but initially this was only faith in himself. The narrative records how he manipulated his father into passing on the blessing to him rather than Esau by scheming and deception. But at least it showed that he wanted the blessing, in contrast to Esau's disregard for what would have been his. Later in his life, God had to 'break' Jacob. He limped for the rest of his life after wrestling with God all night. But this was the turning point for his faith in God. From that moment on he believed God's promises that his 12 boys would become 12 tribes.

These three men, in spite of all their weaknesses and their failures, shine out as men who believed in God. They had faith, in sharp contrast to their relatives, who were people of flesh rather than people of faith.

Lot comes across as a materialist, choosing to go down into the fertile Jordan valley rather than live in the barren hills. He trusted his eyes, while Abraham, with the eyes of faith, knew that God would be with him in the hills. Esau decided he would rather have a bowl of 'instant soup' than the blessing of his father. The letter to the Hebrews tells us not to be like Esau, who regretted his bargain and afterwards sought the blessing with tears, though without genuine repentance. There is, therefore, a stark contrast between the men of faith and their relatives of flesh – a distinction which runs through many families today.

This contrast is also seen in the men's wives. Sarah, Rebekah and Rachel had one thing in common: they were all very beautiful. The three wives of the patriarchs had the lasting beauty of inner character and they all submitted to their husbands. The wives of the others are again a contrast. Lot's wife, for example, looked back to the comfortable life they were leaving but which was going to be judged by God, and having disobeyed God's word was turned into a pillar of salt.

Abraham

Let us look at those three men in greater detail. God made a promise to Abraham on which Christians still rely. God began creation with one man and he began redemption with one man. We are told that God made a covenant with Abraham, a theme which continues through the Bible to Jesus himself, who institutes a new covenant commemorated at the Lord's Supper.

It is important to grasp the meaning of 'covenant' clearly. Some confuse it with the word 'contract', but it is not a bargain struck between two parties of equal power and authority. A covenant is made entirely by one party to bless the other. The other party has only two choices: to accept the terms or to reject them. They cannot change them. When God makes covenants he keeps them and swears by them. Where a human being might say 'by God I promise to do that', God says 'by myself I have sworn', because there is nothing above God to swear by. So he swears by himself and he tells the truth, the whole truth and nothing but the truth.

In his promise to Abraham, God repeats the words of intention 'I will' six times in Genesis 12, rather like a husband marrying a bride. The truth is that the God of the universe married himself to this particular family and his first promise was to give them a place to live in (a little patch of land where the continents meet – the very centre of the world's land mass is Jerusalem and that is where the roads from Africa to Asia and from Arabia to Europe cross, near a little hill called Armageddon in Hebrew, the crossroads of the world). God said, in effect, 'This is the place I am going to give you for

ever.' They hold the title deeds to that place, whatever anybody else says, because God gave the title deeds to them, to
Abraham and his descendants for ever.

His second promise was to give them descendants. He said
there would always be descendants of Abraham on the earth.
And he said this in spite of both Abraham's and Sarah's advanc-
ing years.

The third promise was that he would use them to bless or
to curse every other nation. The calling of the Jews is to share
God with everybody. It is a calling that can cut both ways, for
God said to Abraham, 'Those who curse you will be cursed,
those who bless you will be blessed.' In return God expected
first that every male Jew would be circumcised as a sign that
they were born into that covenant, and second that Abraham
would obey God and do everything God told him to do.

This covenant is at the very heart of the Bible and is the
basis upon which God said, 'I will be your God and you will be
my people', a phrase which is repeated all the way through the
Bible until the very last page in Revelation. It tells us that God
wants to stick with us. At the very end of the Bible God himself
moves out of heaven and comes down to earth to live with us
on a new earth for ever.

Isaac

We know less about him than about his father Abraham or his
son, Jacob, but he is the vital link between them. His faith is to
be seen in his accepting God's choice of a wife, staying in the
land of Canaan when famine struck and leaving the land to his
son even though he did not possess it in fact, only in promise.
Sadly, his loss of sight in old age led to deception by his own
family.

Jacob

Jacob is perhaps the most colourful of the three men. Even when he was being born he was holding the heel of his twin brother Esau, he was grasping from the very beginning. Esau went to live in a place we now call Petra, where it is still possible to view amazing temples carved out of the red sandstone. It was here that Esau formed the nation of Edom. The hatred between Ishmael and Isaac still exists in the Middle East in the tension between Arab and Jew, but the hatred between Esau and Jacob has disappeared. The last Edomites were known by the name of Herod and it was a descendant of Esau who was King of the Jews when Jesus was born. He killed all the babies in Bethlehem to try to get rid of this descendant of Jacob who was born to be King.

Inheritance

Abraham, Isaac and Jacob all showed their faith in one extraordinary, final way. They each left their sons what they did not actually possess. Abraham said to Isaac that he was leaving to him the whole land around them. Isaac also said to Jacob that he was leaving him the whole land, and Jacob said to his 12 boys that he was leaving them the whole land of Canaan. But not one of them possessed what they bequeathed. Only Abraham actually owned any land and this was just the cave at Hebron where Sarah lay buried. They each believed that God had given to them what they were bequeathing, and that one day the whole land would be theirs.

When we read about these men much later in the Bible in Hebrews 11, we discover that 'all these people were still living by faith when they died'. They were all commended for their faith, 'yet none of them received what had been promised. God had planned something better for us so that only together with us would they be made perfect'. Abraham, Isaac and Jacob are not dead. We can see the tombs of their bodies in Hebron, but they are not dead. Jesus said that God *is* the God of Abraham, Isaac and Jacob – not *was* but *is*. He is not the God of dead people: he is the God of the living.

Joseph

The final part of Genesis concerns a story which is familiar to many, the story of Joseph. It is a story that appeals to children as well as adults, a 'goody wins over the baddy' story. It has even been made into a musical, although the popular references to a multicoloured coat are probably inaccurate. It was more likely a coat specifically with long sleeves, rather than any kind of multicoloured garment – the major point being that Joseph was made foreman over the others and wore attire which emphasized that he did not have to do manual work. Such preference was odd since Joseph was not the eldest son, so it led to considerable resentment.

Joseph is the fourth generation, the great-grandson of Abraham, and yet again he is not the eldest. There is a clear pattern here: the natural heir does not receive the blessing. God chooses in his grace who receives it. The pattern has been for it to be one of the younger sons.

In one important way, however, the pattern does not continue. I noted earlier that there is a great difference between Joseph and the previous three generations. God never calls himself 'the God of Joseph'. Angels never appear to Joseph and his brothers are not rejected like those of the other three. His brothers are included in the Godly line of Seth, so there is not the same contrast to be seen in that respect. Furthermore, Joseph is never spoken to directly by God. He receives dreams and is given the interpretation of dreams, but he never actually receives communication from God as the other three patriarchs do.

So it seems that somehow Joseph stands on his own. Why is he different, and why are we told his story?

In part the reason is obvious, for his story links in naturally with the very next book in the Bible. In Exodus we find this family in slavery in Egypt and somehow we need to explain how they got there. The story of Joseph is the vital link, explaining how Jacob and his family migrated down to Egypt for the same reason that Abraham and Isaac had gone down to Egypt earlier: because of a shortage of food. (Egypt does not depend on rain since it has the River Nile flowing down from the Ethiopian highlands, whereas the land of Israel depends for its crops totally on rain brought by the west wind from the Mediterranean.) At the very least, therefore, the story of Joseph is there to link us with the next part of the Bible. The curtain falls after Joseph for some 400 years, about which we know nothing, and when it lifts again the family has become a people of many hundreds of thousands – but now they are slaves in Egypt.

If this is the only reason that the story of Joseph is included in Genesis, then it hardly explains why so much space is given to it. We are told almost as much detail as we are about Abraham and far more than we are about Isaac or Jacob. Why are we told about Joseph in such detail? Is it simply the example of a good man with the moral that good triumphs in the end? Surely there is more to it than that.

There are at least four levels at which we can read the story of Joseph.

1. THE HUMAN ANGLE

The first level is simply the *human* level. It is a vivid story told superbly with very real characters. It is a great adventure, stranger than fiction. There are some extraordinary coincidences in it, and you could summarize Joseph's life in two chapters: Chapter 1, down, and Chapter 2, up. He went all the way down from being the favourite son of his father to becoming a household slave, and he went all the way up from being a forgotten prisoner to being Prime Minister. In between we have the envy of his brothers which brought him low, and the key to a successful ending lying in the dreams. At the human level, therefore, it makes a good musical show for London's West End and thousands see it and enjoy it.

2. GOD'S ANGLE

You can also read the story from *God's* angle. Even though he does not actually talk to Joseph, he is there behind the scenes, the invisible God arranging circumstances for his purposes and plans and revealing them through dreams. It is clear in the Bible that sometimes God needs to speak to his people in this way, but it always needs an interpretation. Joseph said these dreams were from God and that the interpretation would come from God. Daniel would later be noted for the same gift. Joseph believed that his circumstances were overruled by God and that God was behind the things that happened to him.

The key verse in the story of Joseph is found in Chapter 45, verse 7, when he finally made himself known to his brothers after humbling and embarrassing them greatly. Having forgiven them for what they had done to him, he then said, 'But God sent me ahead of you to preserve for you a remnant on earth and to save your lives by a great deliverance.'

Joseph's brothers thought they had got rid of him by selling him to travelling camel traders as a slave and covering his special coat with the blood of a goat to trick their father into believing that his favourite son was dead. Yet Joseph could see that God's hand was in it. He could look back on his work in Egypt, having been elevated to high office following his interpretation of Pharaoh's dream (i.e. there would be seven fat years with good harvest, and seven lean years to follow). By advising that food should be stored during the plentiful years he had actually saved the whole nation of Egypt – and his own family when they also became short of food. He became their saviour.

God's providence can also be seen in the movement of Joseph's family down to Egypt. Although God had promised the land to them, he had told Abraham many years previously that he would have to leave his family in Egypt for 400 years 'until the wickedness of the Amorites was complete'. God would not let the family of Abraham take the promised land from those living in it until they became so dreadful that they forfeited their right to both their land and their lives. God is a moral God: he would not just push one people out and his own people in. Archaeology has indicated to us just how dreadful these people were. Venereal diseases were rife in the land of Canaan because of their corrupt sexual practices. Eventually they reached the point of no return, and only then did God say that his people could have their land. Those who complain about God's injustice in giving that land to the Jews are quite mistaken.

But there were other reasons too. God *wanted* his chosen people to become slaves. It was part of his plan to rescue them from slavery so that they would be grateful to him and live his way, becoming a model for the whole world to see how blessed people are when they live under the government of heaven. So he let them go through the evils of slavery, working seven days a week for no pay, with no land of their own, no money of their own, nothing of their own. Then, as they cried out to him, he reached down and rescued them with his mighty hand. God let it happen for his own purposes. He wanted them to know that it was God who delivered them and gave them their own land.

3. JOSEPH'S CHARACTER

We can also approach the narrative as a study of *Joseph's character*. The remarkable thing is that nothing said about Joseph is bad. We have already noted that the Bible tells the whole truth about Abraham, Isaac and Jacob, who certainly had their weaknesses and sins. Not one word of criticism is levelled at Joseph. The worst thing he did was to be a bit tactless and tell his brothers about his dream of future greatness, but there is no trace whatever of a wrong attitude or reaction in Joseph's character. His reactions as he sinks down the social ladder are first class: there is no trace of resentment, no complaining, no questioning of God, no sense of injustice that he should finish up in prison, on death row in Pharaoh's jail. Furthermore, even though he was far from home and totally unknown, he maintained his integrity when Potiphar's wife tried to seduce him. Even at rock bottom, languishing in jail, his concern seems to have been primarily to help others as he seeks to comfort Pharaoh's cup bearer and baker. Joseph is a man who seems to have no concern for himself, but a deep concern for everyone else.

His character is also flawless when he ascends to be second-in-command of Pharaoh's government. Note his reaction to the brothers who had sold him into slavery. He gives them food and refuses to charge them for it, putting the money back in their sacks. He forgives them with tears, intercedes for them with Pharaoh, and purchases the best land in the Nile delta so that they may live there. They had thrown him out and told his father that he was dead, but here he is providing for their every need.

Joseph is unspoiled either by humiliation or by honour. He is a man of total integrity and the only one so presented in the Old Testament. All the Old Testament characters are presented with their weaknesses as well as their strengths, but here is a man who only has strengths. There is only one other person in the Bible who is like this.

There is one chapter in the middle of the story of Joseph that comes as a shock. It is about his brother Judah. In the middle of the story about this good man there comes a stark contrast with his own brother Judah. Judah visits a woman he thinks is a prostitute, but who is actually his daughter-in-law with a veil on. He takes part in incest and the sordid story is told right in the middle of the Joseph narrative. Why is it there? It is there because it serves to highlight Joseph's integrity by contrast. Just as Abraham was contrasted with Lot, Isaac with Ishmael and Jacob with Esau, so Joseph is contrasted with Judah.

4. A REFLECTION OF JESUS

So far we have discussed this story at three levels: the human story of a man who was taken all the way down to the bottom and then climbed right up to the top, and who became the saviour of his people and the Lord of Egypt; the story of God's overruling of this man's life, using it to save his people; and finally the story of a man of total integrity, who all the way down and all the way up remained a man of truth and honest goodness.

Each level of the story reminds us of another: Jesus himself. Joseph becomes what is known as a *type* of Jesus. 'Type' in this sense means 'foreshadowing'. It is as if God is showing us in the life of Joseph what he is going to do with his own son. Like Joseph, his own son would be rejected by his brethren and taken all the way down to utter humiliation, then raised to be 'Saviour' and 'Lord' of his people.

Once we recognize the 'type', the comparisons are remarkable. The more we read the story of Joseph the more we see this picture of Jesus, as if God knew all along what he was going to do and was giving hints to his people. Jesus himself encouraged the Jews to 'search the Scriptures, for they bear witness of me', referring to the Old Testament. As we read the Old Testament we should always be looking for Jesus, for his likeness, for his shadow. Jesus himself is the substance, but his shadow falls right across the pages of the Old Testament, especially in Genesis.

Jesus in Genesis

Once we have seen that Joseph is a picture of Jesus, we can see Jesus in many other places throughout Genesis. Joseph is a model of God's response to faith in him, and his story demonstrates how God can take a person's life and use him to deliver his people from their need, lifting him up to be Saviour and Lord.

GENEALOGIES

The genealogies in Genesis are in fact the genealogy of our Lord Jesus Christ. If you read Matthew 1 and Luke 3 you will find in the genealogies there names from the book of Genesis. Jesus is of the line of Seth, which comes straight down to the son of Mary. Thus anyone who is in Christ is also reading their own family tree. These are the most important ancestors we have, because through faith in Christ we have become sons of Abraham.

ISAAC

When we examine the characters in Genesis we can see similarities to Jesus. We have noted Joseph already, but let us go back to the time when Abraham was told to offer Isaac as a sacrifice. He was told to go to a specific mountain called Moriah. Years later that same mountain was known as Golgotha, the place where God sacrificed his only son. Genesis 22 tells us that Isaac was Abraham's only beloved son – and we have seen already how Isaac was in his early thirties by then, strong enough to resist his father, but he submitted to being bound and put on the altar.

God stopped Abraham at the crucial point and provided another sacrifice, a ram with its head caught in thorns. Centuries later John the Baptist would say of Jesus, 'Behold the "ram" of God that takes away the sins of the world'. The word 'lamb' is often applied to Jesus, but little, cuddly lambs were never offered for sacrifice – the sacrifices were one-year-old rams with horns. Jesus is depicted in the book of Revelation as the ram with seven horns signifying strength – 'a ram of God'. God provided a ram for Abraham to offer in place of his son, a ram with his head caught in the thorns, and God also announced a new name to himself: 'I am always your provider'. At that same spot another young man in his early thirties was sacrificed with his head caught in thorns. Do you see there a picture of Jesus?

MELCHIZEDEK

It is also worth looking carefully at a strange encounter Abraham had with a man who was both a king and a priest. He was king over the city of Salem (which later became Jerusalem). When Abraham was on his way back from rescuing his family after they had been kidnapped, he arrived with the spoils from the enemy near the city of Salem. This was then a pagan city, nothing to do with Abraham's Godly line. He was met by the strange figure of Melchizedek, who was both a priest and a king, a very unusual combination, never found in Israel. This 'King Priest' brought out bread and wine as refreshments for Abraham and his troops and Abraham gave him a tenth of all the spoils of the battle, a tithe of the treasure. In the New Testament we are told that Jesus is a priest forever in the order of Melchizedek.

JACOB'S LADDER

And what about Jacob's ladder? When Jacob ran away from home he slept outside at night with his head on a stone and dreamt of a ladder (actually more like an escalator). The Hebrew implies that the ladder was moving, and that there was one ladder moving up and one ladder moving down, with angels ascending and descending. Jacob knew that at the top of the ladders was heaven, where God lived.

When he woke he promised to give a tenth of everything he made to God. The giving of tithes was not part of the law until the time of Moses. (Jacob's offer of a tenth of his possessions was more in the nature of a bargain with God: you bring me back home safely and I will give you a tithe. It is not, however, possible to bargain with God – God makes a covenant with you, not the other way round – and Jacob had to learn that the hard way later.)

Centuries later, when Jesus met a man called Nathaniel, he said to Nathaniel, 'I saw you sitting under the fig tree. I noticed you and you are a Jew in whom there is no guile, no deceit.' Nathaniel asked him how he knew this. Jesus replied, 'You think that is wonderful, that I know the details of your life. What will you think if you see angels ascending and descending on the son of man?' He is saying, 'I am Jacob's ladder, I am the link between earth and heaven. I am the new ladder.'

ADAM AND EVE

Further back, in Genesis 3, God made a promise in the middle of his punishment of Adam and Eve. He said to the serpent that the seed – or offspring – of the woman (seed is masculine in the Hebrew) would bruise the serpent's head, even while the serpent bruised the offspring's heel. Bruising a heel is not fatal, but bruising a head is and this is the very first promise that

God would one day deal Satan a fatal blow. We now know who it was who bound the strong man and spoilt his goods.

In Romans 5, Paul tells us that as one man's disobedience brought death, so one man's obedience brought life, implying that Jesus is a second Adam. It was in the Garden of Eden that Adam said 'I won't' and it was in the Garden of Gethsemane that Jesus said 'not my will but yours be done'. What a contrast! They each began a human race: Adam was the first man of the *homo sapiens* race; Jesus was the first of the *homo novus*.

We are all born *homo sapiens*, and through God we can become *homo novus*. The New Testament talks about the new man, the new humanity. There are two human races on earth today: you are either in Adam or you are in Christ. There is a whole new human race and it is going to inhabit a totally new planet earth – indeed a whole new universe.

CREATION

One of the most remarkable things said about Jesus in the New Testament is that he was responsible for the creation of the universe. The early disciples came to see that Jesus was involved in the events of Genesis 1. As John said at the start of his Gospel, 'without him nothing was made that has been made'.

When we read Genesis 1, therefore, we find that Jesus was there. God said, 'Let us make man in our image'. Jesus was part of the plurality of the Godhead.

We have known for several decades now that the earth's surface is on flat plates of rock floating on molten rock, and that these plates are constantly moving, rubbing against each other to cause earthquakes. When it was discovered that these plates moved to form the land masses we have today, the scientists needed to coin a new word for the plates. They called them 'tectonic plates'. In Greek the word *tectone* means 'carpenter'.

The whole planet earth on which we live is the work of a carpenter from Nazareth – and his name is the Lord Jesus Christ!

So we finish our studies in Genesis where we began, with creation. God is indeed answering his problem of what to do when humans rebel. The solution is Jesus Christ, through whom the world came to be, for whom it was made, and by whom we discover the answer to all our questions.

PART II

EXODUS

Introduction

Exodus is the story of the biggest escape in history. Over two million slaves escape from one of the most highly fortified nations in the entire world. It is humanly impossible, an extraordinary story, and it features a series of miracles, including some of the best known in the whole Bible. The leader of the Israelites at the time was a man named Moses. He saw more miracles than Abraham, Isaac and Jacob put together – in some places a number following one after another as God intervened on behalf of his people. Some of the miracles sound a bit like magic, for example when Moses' stick turns into a snake, but most of them are clear manipulations of nature, as God proves his power over all that he has made for the good of his people.

The original Hebrew title for Exodus was 'These are the names', these being the first words of the book to appear on the scroll when the priest came to read them. Our name 'Exodus' comes from the Greek *ex-hodos* – literally *ex*: 'out', *hoddos*: 'way' (similar to the Latin word *exit*), 'the way out'.

The whole event of the Exodus had a profound significance on two fronts.

1. National

First, it had national significance for the people of Israel. It marked the beginning of their national history. They received their political freedom and became a sovereign nation in their own right. Though they did not yet have a land they were a nation with a name of their own: 'Israel'. So central was this event that ever since then its celebration has been written into their national calendar. Just as Americans celebrate their independence on 4 July, so every March/April the Jews celebrate the Exodus. They eat the Passover meal and recount the mighty acts of God.

2. Spiritual

Second, it had spiritual significance. The Israelites discovered that their God was the God who made the whole universe and could control what he had made for their sake. They came to believe that their God was more powerful than all the gods of Egypt put together. Later they would come to realize that their God was the only God who existed (see especially the prophecies of Isaiah).

The truth that God was more powerful than every other god was made clear by the name which God gave to himself. His 'formal' title was El-Shaddai, God Almighty, but it is in the book of Exodus that the nation was given his personal name. Just as knowing a person's name enables a human relationship to become more intimate, when they discovered God's name Israel could enter into a more intimate relationship with him.

In English we translate the name as 'Yahweh', though there are no vowels in the Hebrew – strictly speaking it should simply be Y H W H. The name is a participle of the verb 'to be'. We saw in our study of Genesis that 'always' is an English word which communicates how the Jews would have understood it.

God is the eternal one without beginning or end – 'always'. This is his first name, but he has many second names too: 'Always my provider', 'Always my helper', 'Always my protector', 'Always my healer'.

In the book of Exodus we are also presented with the extraordinary truth that the creator of everything becomes the redeemer of a few people. The word 'redemption' includes the idea of releasing the kidnapped when the ransom price has been paid. This is how Israel was to understand her God. He was the creator of the universe and also the redeemer of his people. Both aspects are important if we are to learn to know God as he is revealed in the Bible.

The book

Exodus is one of the five books which Moses wrote. Genesis deals with events before his lifetime and Exodus, Leviticus, Numbers and Deuteronomy tell of events during his lifetime. These books are crucial to the life of Israel as they record the foundations of the nation. They are also foundational to the whole Old Testament. This group of slaves needed to know who they were and how they came to be a nation.

We saw in our study of Genesis how Moses collected two things from the people's memories: *genealogies* and *stories about their ancestors*. The book of Genesis is entirely made up of such memories. Exodus, Leviticus, Numbers and Deuteronomy are different, comprising a mixture of narrative and legislation. The narrative describes the Israelites' move from Egypt through the wilderness and into the land of Canaan. The legislation reflects what God said to them concerning how they should live. It is this unique combination of narrative and legislation that characterizes these other four books of Moses.

Exodus itself is part narrative and part legislation. The first half details what God did on the Israelites' behalf to get them out of slavery. The second half describes what God said about how they were to live now that they were free. The first half demonstrates God's grace towards them in getting them out of their problems. The second half shows that God expects them to show their gratitude for that grace by living his way. This emphasis is important. Too many people read the law of Moses thinking that it shows how they can be accepted by God. They get it the wrong way round. The people of Israel were redeemed by God, *then* they were given the law to keep as an expression of gratitude. This principle is the same in the New Testament: Christians are redeemed and *then* told how to live holy lives. To use theological jargon, justification comes before sanctification. We do not become Christians by living right first, but by being redeemed and liberated and then living right. *The liberation comes before the legislation*.

In Exodus the Israelites' liberation takes place in Egypt and the legislation takes place at Mount Sinai, as they travel to Canaan. Here they respond to God's covenant commitment to them. The covenant takes the form of a wedding service. God says 'I will' (be your God if you obey me) and then the people have to say 'We will' (be your people and obey you).

STRUCTURE

As well as there being two halves to the book of Exodus, there are ten different portions within it: six sections in Chapters 1–18 and four in Chapters 19–40. They can be arranged as shown in the following table.

Chapters 1–18
(people mobile)
Key themes
DIVINE DEEDS
GRACE
LIBERATION
FROM EGYPT
SLAVERY(men)
REDEMPTION

Chapters 19–40
(people stationary)
Key themes
DIVINE WORDS
GRATITUDE
LEGISLATION
TO SINAI
SERVICE (God)
RIGHTEOUSNESS

The sections
1. **1** Multiplication and murder

(ISRAEL)
2. **2–3** Bulrushes and burning bush
(MOSES)
3. **5–11** Plague and pestilence

(PHARAOH)
4. **12–13:16** Feast and first-born

(PASSOVER)
5. **13:17–15:21** Delivered and drowned
(RED SEA)
6. **15:22–18:27** Provided and protected
(WILDERNESS)

The sections
7. **19–24** Commandments and covenant
(SINAI)
8. **25–31** Specification and specialists
(TABERNACLE)
9. **32–34** Indulgence and intercession
(GOLDEN CALF)
10. **35–40** Construction and consecration
(TABERNACLE)

The first part (Chapters 1–18) details the events preceding and following their flight from Egypt. It includes many miracles, including the most famous, how the Israelites were protected when the first-born of Egypt were killed, and how they were able to pass through the Red Sea. It also includes the less famous but no less remarkable provision of God as they journey from Egypt to Sinai. During the Yom Kippur war of 1973 the Egyptian army was unable to last more than three days in the desert, yet in Exodus 2.5 million people survived there for 40 years.

In the second part the focus is on legislation. The Ten Commandments appear first, but there is also other legislation concerned with God's intention to live among his people. Just as they lived in tents, so God would join them in their camp. But his own tent would be distinct and separate from theirs. These people had never made anything but mud bricks until that point, but God gave them the skills to work with gold, silver and wood.

The second part does also include some narrative. Here we read the saddest part of the whole book, as the people indulge themselves and make a golden calf to worship. The book finishes with the construction of the tabernacle. God takes up residence and the glory comes down on his tent.

Chapters 1–18

Many perceive the first part of Exodus to be full of problems because it is such an unnatural story. There are so many extraordinary events that many people suggest that what we have here is a series of legends rather than truth. So, are the events described part of a myth or a miracle?

Myth or miracle?

1. NO SECULAR RECORD

The problem is not just with the nature of the events themselves, but also with the fact that the events are not backed up by any secular, historical record. All we have is just one mention of 'the habiru' in Goshen – a possible reference to the 'Hebrews', as the 'children of Israel' were known. This lack of documentation should not surprise us, however. The Exodus of the Jews was one of the most humiliating events in Egypt's experience. They suffered severe plagues, including the death of their first-born. Their best charioteers were drowned in the Red Sea. This hardly made for comforting reflection.

2. THE NUMBERS INVOLVED

Many people find the story hard to believe due to the large numbers involved. We are told there were 2.5 million slaves who left Egypt. By any reckoning this is a huge number. If they marched five abreast, the column would be about 110 miles long, and that does not include the livestock. It would take months for them to move anywhere. It is also a huge population to keep fed and watered in a desert for 40 years.

3. THE DATE

There is also a question about the dating of the events. As we have no other record outside the Bible we cannot date the events with any certainty. So we do not know for sure which Pharaoh was involved and when it all took place. The choice seems to be between Rameses II, who had a powerful military force, who erected huge statues of himself and whose sons' tomb has only recently been discovered, and Dudimore, according to the 'new chronology' of David M. Rohl.*

(see footnote overleaf).

4. THE ROUTE

There is controversy concerning the route which the Israelites took when they left Egypt, too. There are three possibilities to consider: a route to the north, a route to the south, or one through the middle. We will come back to this question on page 99.

5. THE DIVINE NAME

Other scholars find problems with God's words to Moses in Exodus 6:3 where he says: 'I am the LORD. I appeared to Abraham, to Isaac and to Jacob as God Almighty, but by my name the LORD I did not make myself known to them.'

That last phrase may either be a statement ('...I did not make myself known...'), in which case Abraham knew him as 'God', but without a personal name distinguishing him from other gods; or as a question ('...did I not make myself known...?'), in which case Abraham knew God by name as well as Moses. The latter is less likely.

THE FACTS

All these questions have made scholars doubt whether they are reading fact, fiction or perhaps 'faction'. Those who do not believe the events need to ask why they cannot. Is it prejudice or a so-called scientific view of the universe which prevents them believing? At the same time we can also try to look for the most understandable explanation for the facts which are indisputable.

1. Nobody can dispute that there is a nation called Israel in the world today. So where did they come from? How did

---

* See *A Test of Time* (BCA, 1996), and *Legend* (BCA, 1988) for this Egyptologist's remarkable claims to have discovered evidence for Joseph's time in Egypt, Moses' liberation and, even further back, the location of the Garden of Eden!

they get started? How did they ever become a nation if they were originally a bunch of slaves? We do know from secular records that they were a bunch of slaves. Something dramatic is needed to explain the existence of Israel.

2. Every year, every Jewish family celebrates the Passover. Why do they do it? This is a ritual which has survived for many thousands of years and also needs some explanation.

These two known facts at least need explanation, therefore, and it is the book of Exodus which provides the answers. So let us look at each section, following the structure laid out in the table above, and consider some of the questions surrounding the text.

1. Multiplication and murder

In this opening section we discover that the number of Hebrew slaves must have been around 2.5 million by the time the Exodus narrative starts. This may seem a large number given that they started with just the 12 sons of Jacob, their offspring and wider family. But if each family had four children (not a large number in those days) over 30 generations then this number could be achieved.

But why did they stay in Egypt for 400 years when they only went there for seven originally? They first arrived in the time of Joseph and Jacob following a famine in Canaan. (Egypt was the bread-basket of the Middle East thanks to Joseph's judicious storing of grain during the seven years of plenty.) They arrive voluntarily, are accepted as guests of the government and are given a fertile piece of the Nile delta called Goshen to live on together. So they remain a nation during the seven years of famine. But at the end of that time why did they not go back to their own land? This is a pertinent question, given that they are eventually forced to become slaves in Egypt.

The human reason is that they were very comfortable. It was much easier to make a living in the Nile delta than it was on the hills of Judea. The land was fertile, the climate was warmer, with no snow in winter as there was in the hills of Judea. The diet was good, they could eat fish from the Nile and look after themselves far better. So they stayed because they were comfortable. It was only when they were forced to become slaves that they remembered God and started crying out to him.

There is also a divine reason. God did not do anything to encourage them to go back to their own land for 400 years. If they had returned as soon as the famine was over, they would have been only a few people, far too small a number to accomplish what God intended. For it was God's intention to remove the people of Canaan from the land. He explained to Abraham that his descendants would stay in Egypt until the wickedness of the Canaanites was completed. God had to wait until they became so bad that it would be an act of justice and judgement to throw them out of the Promised Land and let the Hebrew slaves in. We read in Deuteronomy that it was not any virtue on the part of the Israelites which made God choose them. Indeed, if they behaved in the land like those they had expelled, they too would have to leave. To be instruments of justice they had to be righteous themselves.

But all that was to come later. As slaves in Egypt, the people of Israel faced three oppressive decrees:

1. Forced labour: the Pharaoh decided to use the Hebrews as labour for his building programmes.

2. Tougher conditions: they had to make bricks without straw (which meant the bricks were much heavier to carry). Archaeological digs within Egypt have discovered buildings made of three different types of brick: the foundations with straw, the middle with rubbish, as the Hebrews sought to continue making light bricks once denied the straw, and then on the top bricks made entirely of clay. The idea behind this harsh decree was that the extra weight of the bricks would make the Hebrews too tired for sex or mischief and so their population would decrease. It was a crude form of population control and it did not work, so the Egyptians had to introduce a third decree.

3. Death: all the baby boys born to the Hebrew slaves had to be thrown to the crocodiles in the River Nile.

2. Bulrushes and the burning bush

Most people know this story well. The River Nile was full of crocodiles and this form of genocide was considered necessary by the Egyptians if Israelite numbers were to be effectively reduced. The baby Moses should have died in this way. But we note that under God's providence Moses, like Joseph, was brought up at court and given the best education at the Egyptian university. This, of course, made him far better educated than any of the Hebrew slaves, and enabled him to write the first five books of the Bible. For the Jews Moses was the second greatest man in Old Testament – after Abraham. His time as an Egyptian prince came to a sudden end, however, when he lost his temper with one of the Egyptian slave drivers and killed him, after which he had to flee for his life.

The statistics of Moses' life make interesting reading. At the age of 40, he spent 40 years tending sheep in the very wilderness to which he would return to live for 40 years with the people of Israel! This was clearly God's hand at work.

Moses' meeting with the Lord through the burning bush is also intriguing, not so much for the bush as for Moses' excuses. God first told Moses to take off his shoes because he was on holy ground. Then he told Moses that he was going to be the man to draw God's people out of Egypt. Moses made five excuses as to why he should not do it.

First he said he was *insignificant*. God said he would be with him – he was the important one. Next he said that he was *ignorant* and had nothing to say. God told him that he would tell Moses what to say. His third excuse was that he would be *impotent* to convince the people that God had met with him and told him to lead them. God said that his power was going to be with Moses and he would perform miracles. Then Moses said that he was *incompetent* at speaking, having a stammer which would prevent him putting words together. So God provided his brother Aaron to be his spokesman. God would tell Moses what to say and he would relay it to Aaron. Finally Moses said that he was *irrelevant* – please would God send someone else? But God had provided Aaron as a partner: they would work together. Each time Moses' questioning focuses upon his weakness, and each time God has an answer.

3. Plague and pestilence

Ten plagues are mentioned in this section: the Nile turned to blood, the plague of frogs, the plague of gnats and mosquitoes, the plague of flies, the cattle disease, the boils, the hail storm, the plague of locusts, the darkness over the land and, finally, the death of the first-born.

There are a number of things to notice, and the first is that God is in total control of the insect world. God can tell mosquitoes and locusts what to do and where to go, just as he can tell frogs what to do. The plagues give a tremendous sense of God's control over what he has created.

It is also interesting to note how the plagues increase in intensity. There is a build-up from discomfort to disease to danger to death. There is also a movement from plagues affecting nature to plagues affecting people. The afflictions gradually get worse as Pharaoh and the Egyptian people refuse to respond to the warnings. Some see the final punishment as unfair – is the killing of the first-born not far too excessive and harsh? But the Egyptians had done worse to the Israelites, killing all their baby boys, so this retribution was thoroughly appropriate.

It is easy, too, to miss the religious contest that takes place during the plagues. Every one of those plagues was an attack on a particular god worshipped by the Egyptians:

Khuum: the guardian of the Nile
Hapi: the spirit of the Nile
Osiris: the Nile was believed to be the bloodstream of Osiris
Heqt: a frog-like god of resurrection
Hathor: a mother goddess who was a cow
Apis: a bull of the god Ptah, a symbol of fertility
Minevis: also a bull, the sacred bull of Heliopolis
Imhotep: the god of medicine
Nut: the sky goddess
Seth: the protector of crops
Re, Aten, Atum and Horus: all sun gods
Pharaoh was also said to be divine

The plagues were specifically directed against these Egyptian gods. The message was very simple: the God of the Hebrew slaves is far more powerful than all your gods put together.

Some see a problem with what we are told in this section of narrative about Pharaoh's heart. We read that God hardened Pharaoh's heart. Some have even erected a doctrine of predestination on this passage and verses in Romans 9 where Paul talks about God hardening Pharaoh's heart. They suggest that the passage teaches that it is up to God to choose whether he softens or hardens someone's heart. Advocates of this view argue that we do not know why God makes these choices, but whatever the reason, in the case of Pharaoh he decided he was going to harden his heart. It is as if God picks names out of a hat and decides to save some and send others to hell, to harden some and soften others.

This is not what the Bible teaches, however. If you study the text carefully you find that Pharaoh's heart was hardened ten times. On the first seven occasions Pharaoh hardens his own heart, in the next three God hardens Pharaoh's heart. So God only hardens Pharaoh's heart after Pharaoh has deliberately and repeatedly hardened his own heart. He confirms the choice that Pharaoh has made. This is the way God punishes: he helps people along the road they are determined to travel. In Revelation God says, 'Let him that is filthy be filthy still.' So there is no arbitrary choice about God's dealings with Pharaoh – he hardens his own heart first and then God hardens it for him. God responds to our choices. If we persistently choose the wrong way, God will help us along that route. He will demonstrate his judgement if we refuse to be a demonstration of his mercy.

4. Feast and first-born

The tenth plague was that every first-born boy in every Egyptian family would die. This was the pivotal plague to the whole drama. The tragedy would also happen to the Jews unless they followed God's instructions. They were to paint the blood of a lamb on their doorposts. The angel of death would come to Egypt that night and pass over the houses displaying the mark. For the other households, death would take place at midnight. Interestingly, blood is a scarlet/maroon colour, the hardest colour to see in the dark.

The blood had additional significance: the Jews were to slaughter a one-year-old ram, fully mature, and after they had put its blood on their doorposts they were to take it inside for roasting. So they were both covered by it and fed by it. When we call Jesus the 'lamb of God' it can suggest a softer, more docile image than the Bible intends, for he is actually the 'ram of God', which gives a more robust picture. The Jews were to eat the meat standing up, dressed and ready to leave at a moment's notice. They were told to take emergency rations of unleavened bread. They were to leave Egypt that very night.

The Jews continue to keep the feast of the Passover to this day. At a particular moment in the evening, the youngest member of the family has to ask, 'What does all this mean?' The oldest member of the family replies, 'This is what God did on the night when every first-born boy died and we were saved because of the blood of the ram.' Thus they are reminded that the first-born needs to be redeemed in every generation.

5. Delivered and drowned

There are three possibilities for the route taken by the Israelites when they left Egypt, indicated on the map overleaf.

The first is known as the northern route. This suggests that they went through a row of sandbanks in a shallow part of the Mediterranean. Maps of Egypt show sandbanks marked at a place called Lake Sirbonis. Their route then takes them to Kadesh Barnea. But they could not have been followed by the Egyptian chariots across the sandbanks, so this seems unlikely.

The second theory is that they went straight across through the Mitler Pass to Kadesh. But there was a line of fortresses (where the Suez Canal is today) built across there, against any invasion from the east. So the Israelites would have

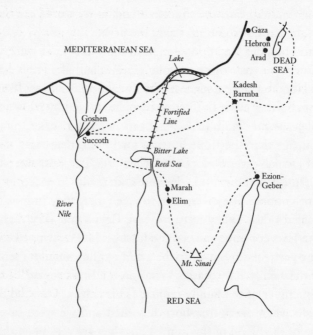

had to get through that line of fortresses. They were not armed and able to fight, so this route is very unlikely also.

The third possibility was the southern route down to Mount Sinai, where Moses had been a shepherd for 40 years. This is the most likely, for Moses knew this country. The location of Mount Sinai is uncertain, but all the tradition in the Middle East puts Sinai in the south. The Israelites left Goshen and came south. Pharaoh would only let them go into the desert, thinking that he could always bring them back from there. Having camped, they were hidden from the Egyptians by a cloud God had sent.

As regards the actual crossing of the sea, the Bible does not say that God divided the Red Sea, but that he sent an east wind which divided the Red Sea. But how could an east wind divide a sea?

If we were to examine the area in detail we would see that years ago the Great Bitter Lakes were actually joined up to what we call the Red Sea (see diagram below). They were joined up by a shallow, marshy channel called the 'Reed Sea' and in fact the Hebrew suggests the 'Reed Sea' is a more likely name than the 'Red Sea'. The fortified line came right down to the Bitter Lake.

If this was where the Hebrews crossed, there are two natural forces which could have divided the sea. A strong east wind could drive the water to the west end of the Great Bitter Lake, an ebb tide also pulling it south.

This does not explain the miracle at all. How did the east wind just happen to come at the right time? In looking at it in such a down-to-earth way, we are not trying to explain away the miracle. Rather we are showing that it is a miracle of 'coincidence'. In fact, the Bible tells us that there is no such thing as 'coincidence', but only 'providence'.

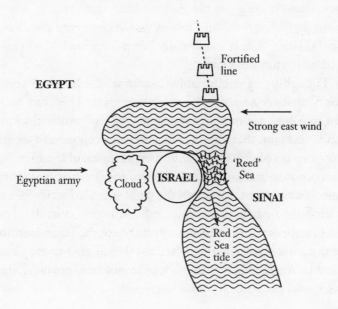

The most striking fact about this crossing of the Red Sea or Reed Sea is that it happened on the third day after the Passover lamb was killed. The Israelites' liberation came on the third day after the Passover lamb. Furthermore, the book of Exodus tells us the very hour when the Passover lamb had to be slaughtered: 3.00 p.m. On the third day after that the Israelites finally escape. They are free of Pharaoh and will never see him again. We will note later some parallels with events in the New Testament.

6. Provided and protected

The desert region over which the Israelites travelled was unable to support human life. It was not the ideal place to take 2.5 million people plus animals.

There were both external and internal problems for Moses, therefore, the most basic being the physical need for food and water. Every morning God provided food for them. They found it lying on the ground when they awoke. It was known as 'What is it?' in Hebrew – *Manna*. Every day there were 900 tons of it. It was literally bread from heaven, a theme revisited later in the Bible.

Though living comfortably on manna, the Israelites complained that they were not getting any meat. They had been used to a high-protein diet in Egypt. So God sent a flock of quails, so many that they lay 1.5 metres deep on the desert floor. The people ate quails until they were sick of them!

They also had a problem with water. The first oasis they came to was Marah. Although the place provided water, it was undrinkable – until it became fresh through a miracle. The next place, Elim, had fresh water from the start. The quantities required were considerable – at least 2 million gallons a day would be needed for that number of animals and people. Later they would get water from rock reservoirs. Perhaps one of the biggest miracles of their providential journey was that their sandals never wore out. Rocks even today wreck rubber tyres on vehicles, yet these sandals lasted 40 years!

Moses also faced internal difficulties. Given the enormous numbers, it is no wonder that one of the biggest problems Moses had was judging disputes between the people. We are told that this could go on all day, to the point where Moses became exhausted. It needed his father-in-law Jethro to suggest a delegation of responsibility, whereby Moses appointed 70 elders to assist in the work.

Chapters 19–40

After the narrative of the escape from Egypt, the second part of Exodus turns more towards legislation, the commandments God gave his people, telling them how they were to live, and the covenant he made with them.

7. Commandments and covenant

There are three 'legal' collections in the second half of Exodus. The best known is the 'Ten Commandments' (or decalogue, which means '10 words'), written with God's finger on two tablets of stone. (Most modern pictures of the event depict Moses returning from Mount Sinai with the Ten Commandments split between the two tablets, five on one and five on the other, but actually all 10 were on each stone.) This was a legal contract, in keeping with similar treaties agreed at that time. A conquering king might make a treaty with a vanquished nation, for example. Each party would have a copy. In the case of the Ten Commandments, one copy was God's and one copy was the people's. This treaty was special, however, known in the Bible as a 'covenant'. A covenant was not a *bargain* between two parties but a *contract* written by God which could be either accepted or rejected by the people.

The Ten Commandments formed the first legal collection and this was followed by what is known as the 'Book of the Covenant', which can be found in Exodus 20:23–23:33. This deals with laws relating to community life. The third collection is the book of laws in Chapters 25–31, which centre on the worshipping life of Israel and are concerned with the place of worship and those conducting worship. Overlap and expansion of these laws is found in Deuteronomy. Thus there are not just Ten Commandments, but a total of 613 rules and regulations about the way to live right before God.

It is crucial to underline the importance of the *context* of the laws in Exodus. The Ten Commandments and the Book of the Covenant are sandwiched between two links which refer to the past and the future.

1. In 20:2 God says, 'I am the LORD your God, who brought you out of Egypt, out of the land of slavery.'
2. In 23:20–33 God assures the people of his presence in the future and of the provision of land, providing they keep to his ways.

The first text refers back to Egypt and the second passage focuses on entering Canaan in the future. The context tells us that these laws from God are for people who have experienced his *past* and are expecting his *future* and who will therefore be able to live in his *present*.

King Alfred based the British legal system on the Ten Commandments, but it is hard to see how people can under-stand them if they have not experienced redemption. They must be seen in the proper context.

THE TEN COMMANDMENTS

A closer look at the Ten Commandments and the accompanying legislation reveals three basic principles which are enshrined there. First is the principle of **respect**. All the Ten Commandments are based on this – respect for God, respect for his name, respect for his day, respect for people, respect for family life, respect for life itself, respect for marriage, respect for people's property, respect for people's reputation.

The message is clear: a healthy, holy society is built on respect. So much of society today, especially the mass media, sets out to destroy respect. Television comedy often encourages an irreverent view of life so that nothing is regarded as sacred. Everything and everyone is a potential figure of fun. But it is clear that the loss of respect for God leads to idolatry, and the loss of respect for people leads to immorality and injustice.

Most of the Ten Commandments are about acts or words, but the last of the ten is about feelings – it is the only one about the heart. Perhaps this is why the apostle Paul said in Romans 7 that he had kept the first nine but he could not manage the tenth, the commandment about greed. For when we desire something we do not have, our problem is with our inner life. If you break one law you have broken them all. They all belong together like a necklace, and if you break a necklace just once the beads are all lost. In reality there are not ten separate commandments. They are all one law.

The second principle is **responsibility**. Increasingly we are taught that we are not responsible for our actions, even down to the claim that wickedness is due to genetics! We know that original sin is transferred through the genes, but the idea that some people are more wicked than others because they have a wrong gene leads to the view that people are not responsible for what they do. Exodus stands directly opposed to that view.

The Lord God says we are responsible before him for how we live with regard to his law.

The third principle is **retribution**. There are three reasons for punishment under the law. The first is *reformation*: punishment is intended to make the wrongdoer better. The second is *deterrence*: the idea being that observing others being punished works as a warning to other would-be malefactors. The third is *retribution*: the punishment occurs simply because the person deserves it, with no necessary concern for whether others heed the warning or the guilty party learns from his errors. This third principle of retribution is enshrined in the Exodus laws.

Capital punishment is applied to 18 different sins against God, from murder to breaking the Sabbath. These also include kidnapping, cursing or assaulting parents, and occasions when a person's uncontrolled animal causes death.

There is a very careful distinction in God's law between *intentional* and *accidental* death. There are two sorts of killing: intentional murder and accidental manslaughter. One carries the death penalty, the other a less severe punishment. In every case we are told that there is no sacrifice in the Mosaic law for continued deliberate, intentional sin. Indeed, if you read Hebrews you will find the same thing being said in the New Testament.

It is worth noting that the denial of personal freedom through imprisonment is not an option under the law. Nowhere in the Bible is this form of punishment argued. There was, however, a clear system of *restitution*, a system of compensation for those who had been injured. This is the *lex talionis*, known today by the shorthand expression 'an eye for an eye and a tooth for a tooth'. If, for example, a pregnant woman is attacked and the baby she carries is born with a deformity resulting from the attack, the guilty party will be handicapped in the same way as the victim. In other cases there was a system of repayment in kind or cash when property was damaged or stolen.

8. Specification and specialists

SPECIFICATIONS

Next we come to the extraordinary fact that God wanted to live with Israel. He had already made his holiness very clear. When the law was given on Mount Sinai, God wanted the Israelites to be sure what his holiness meant. God said that no one could touch his holy mountain and live. Moses erected a fence around the bottom. The giving of the law was accompanied by thunder, lightning and fire, indicating God's power and separateness from man.

But having emphasized his separateness, God then tells Moses that he wants to come down and live in the camp with them. Wherever they camp he wants to be there at the heart of his people. It will be in a tent in the middle of the camp and it must be a tent which communicates his holiness, so that the people will worship him respectfully.

This tent was called the 'tabernacle' and Exodus gives us the building specifications which God laid down, in the laws concerning the religious life of Israel (Chapters 25–31). Everything about the tabernacle was to speak of God and the right approach to him. It was to be located in the centre of the camp, with the 12 tribes arranged in sequence around it.

SPECIALISTS

To use it

Most importantly, the tabernacle was not readily accessible, despite being in the middle of the camp. To begin with there was a fence 100 cubits by 25, high enough to prevent an outsider looking in. The fence had just one opening situated

The Tabernacle

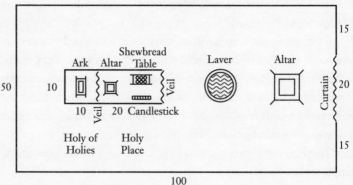

opposite the tribe of Judah. Inside the fence was a courtyard with an *altar* and a *laver*.

The first approach to God, therefore, would be through sacrifice: the animal would be slaughtered and then burnt on the altar in offering to the Lord. Then the worshipper would cleanse his hands in the copper laver between the altar and the holy place. Only then could God's tent be approached. The tent had two sections, the place where God actually lived being a smaller part of the larger tent, a place shut off from human view and visited just once a year by the High Priest.

The larger tent was 10 yards by 30 yards and was known as the *holy place*. Only priests were allowed to enter and then only if they had sacrificed an animal and cleansed their hands in the laver. It had three pieces of furniture. There was a table with *shewbread*, 12 loaves representing the 12 tribes of Israel. There was also a seven-branch candlestick lit by holy oil burning continually, and another altar for sacrifice next to a veil.

The veil hid an area 10 yards by 10 yards, *the holy of holies*: the place where God dwelt. In the holy of holies was a chest and above the chest were two cherubim. In the Bible, cherubim are always angels of judgement. Here they are described as looking downwards to the golden top of the mercy seat. Once a year the High Priest would enter the holy of holies and sacrifice a one-year-old, spotless ram as atonement for the people. Also located in the holy of holies was the ark of the covenant, containing some manna and the books of the law. There was no natural light within the holy of holies, yet it was always radiantly bright. God dwelt there and his glory lit the place.

The beauty of the tabernacle must have been breathtaking, but most of it was hidden. There were beautifully embroidered curtains and coverings, but all were covered with a badger's skin, hiding the beauty from the people. Inside were golden pieces of furniture and curtains embroidered in blue (the colour of heaven), red (the colour of blood), silver and gold.

The whole structure indicated that if you wished to come to God you must make a sacrifice first in order to be clean. God said that this was a copy of where he lived in heaven.

Even when this tent was dismantled and moved, all the elements were kept covered up. The tent had to be carried by specified people and the 'ordinary' people had to keep a thousand paces away from it until it was erected again.

The holiness of God is also emphasized in the clothes of the priests. The High Priest was given specific instructions regarding what he was to wear. He wore 12 jewels on his chest representing the 12 tribes of Israel. These jewels are mentioned again on the last page of the Bible, which describes the New Jerusalem. The High Priest also wore a special girdle, turban, robe, ephod and coat.

The ordinary priests also had 'robes of office', but their requirements included only special coats, girdles, caps and breeches. We can discern in these different robes a picture of the one to come who would be the High Priest for ever on behalf of his people.

To build it

Up to that point, the people's skills consisted only of constructing and transporting bricks, so the task of building such an elaborate tent would normally have been beyond them. We are told that Bezalel, Oholiab and others were given particular gifts by God to accomplish the building. This is the first mention of 'spiritual gifts' in the Bible, and it is interesting that it should be in association with manual tasks such as these.

9. Indulgence and intercession

INDULGENCE

Moses was on Mount Sinai for a long time receiving the law. Not knowing what had happened to him, the people asked Aaron if they could worship a 'god' they could see. So with Aaron's help they melted down their gold to make a bull calf they could worship. The choice of animal was significant. As we have already noted, these animals were one of many idols used by the Egyptians. Bulls and calves were symbols of fertility and have been used as such down through history. It is a clear principle of Scripture that idolatry leads to immorality: loss of respect for God leads to loss of respect for people. A wild orgy followed. When Moses came down and saw what was going on, he smashed both copies of the law. He was symbolizing what the people had already done by their behaviour.

INTERCESSION

Moses went back up the mountain and told God that he was fed up with the people, only to find that God was feeling just the same. We reach a key moment in the history of Israel and a pivotal moment in Moses' leadership. Moses told God that if he was going to blot Israel out of his book, he should be blotted out too, as he did not want to be the only one left. He was effectively saying, 'Take my life in atonement for them.' God explained that he only blots out of his book the names of those who have sinned against him, a theme picked up at various points throughout the Bible. The most important thing in life is to keep your name in the Book of Life. God said to Moses, 'I blot out of my book those who sin against me.'

Moses insisted that the people were punished and God told him to deal with the ringleaders. Three thousand died. This precise figure may mean little to us, but the details of the Exodus narrative have some amazing correspondences with events in the New Testament. The law was given on Sinai on the fiftieth day after the Passover lamb was killed. The lamb was killed at 3.00 p.m. and on the third day after that the slaves were liberated. On the fiftieth day after the Passover the law was given, a day the Jews then called Pentecost. Three thousand people died because they broke the law. It was on that same fiftieth day centuries later, when the Jews were celebrating the giving of the law, that God gave his Spirit – and this time 3,000 people were saved (see Acts 2).

10. Construction and consecration

Where did the Israelites get all the materials they needed to build the tabernacle? At least one ton of gold was needed, not to mention the cloth, linen, jewels, copper and wood. There was an average gift of a fifth of an ounce of gold from each man.

God had told Abraham many centuries before that not only would his descendants be in slavery, but when they left the land of their captivity he would bring them out with great possessions. The materials for the tabernacle and the priests' garments actually came from the Egyptians, who were so glad to see the back of the Israelites that they gave them all their jewellery. This tells us how they came to *have* the materials. They came to be *used* in the tabernacle because the people gave them, donated them for use in this way. Four words describe the nature of their giving: it was spontaneous, thoughtful, regular and sacrificial. This was not an enforced collection with penalties for those who did not give, but was purely down to the free decision of the people ('Everyone who is willing...').

At the end of Exodus we are told how God took up residence and consecrated the tent. The people saw his glory arrive and they saw the plume of smoke or cloud above the inner room. The inner room became filled with light as the glory of the Lord came into it. God was camping with his people. Thereafter, when they saw the cloud and the light move they knew it was time to move on.

Christian use of the Book of Exodus

The story of Exodus is compelling and the details of the Israelites' worship fascinating, but we must ask this: How should Christians read it today?

The first thing to say is that God has not changed. He deals with Christians in the same way as he did with the children of Israel. That is why so many of the words in Exodus are used again in the New Testament – words such as law, covenant, blood, lamb, Passover, Exodus, leaven. They are used in the New Testament but derive their meaning from the book of Exodus.

At the same time there are some significant differences. We are not now under the law of Moses but under the law of Christ. As we shall see, in some ways this makes things harder and in other ways it makes them easier.

The tabernacle is no longer necessary, for we know that Christ has provided direct access into the holy of holies. Neither are we dependent on God's provision of food and water from the sky and the rock.

There are two essential ways in which Christians need to apply Exodus today.

Christ

Christians are to seek Christ in the book of Exodus. Jesus said, 'Search the Scriptures, for they bear witness to me.' The Exodus is central to the Old Testament, and all the books which follow look back to it as the redemption on which everything else is based. In the same way the cross is central to the New Testament.

This is not a fanciful connection. Six months before Jesus died on the cross he was 4,000 feet high on top of Mount Hermon in the north of Israel, talking with Moses and Elijah. Luke's Gospel tells us that they talked about 'the exodus' which Jesus was about to accomplish in Jerusalem.

What is more, Jesus died at 3.00 p.m., the very time when thousands of Passover lambs were being slaughtered. So Christ is called 'our Passover lamb', the one who has been sacrificed for us so that the angel of death would pass over those who trust in him. He rose from the dead on the third day and his resurrection liberates us from death, just as the Hebrews were liberated from slavery on the third day after the Passover.

There are other links, too. We read in John's Gospel that Jesus is the bread from heaven. Paul says that Jesus is the rock from which Moses drew the water for the children of Israel. John also says in his Gospel that 'the word became flesh and "tabernacled among us"'. He literally pitched his tent, God in Christ dwelling in the midst of his people.

With all this in mind, we can understand Christ's words in Matthew: 'I did not come to destroy the law but to fulfil it'. In short, we cannot understand the New Testament without the Old.

Christians

The book of Exodus can also be applied to Christians. Paul, reflecting on some of the events in Exodus, writes to the church at Corinth: 'These things occurred as examples, to keep us from setting our hearts on evil things, as they did.'

The crossing of the Red Sea prefigures baptism. Paul says the children of Israel were baptized into Moses in the Red Sea and his readers had been baptized into Christ.

Christians also have a Passover meal regularly, for the Lord's Supper is a Passover meal, commemorating the liberation of Christ.

Paul speaks of keeping the feast and getting rid of the yeast or leaven because Christ the Passover lamb has been sacrificed. This seems a strange exhortation until we consider the context. He was writing to a church about the immoral behaviour of a believer who was sleeping with his stepmother. In this context the yeast stood for the evil that was taking place which needed to be got rid of if they were truly to 'keep the feast'. The Exodus account sees things in a material way, while the New Testament sees them in a moral context.

Many become especially concerned about how Christians should treat the laws given to Moses. It is true that we do not need to keep the law, but in many ways the 'Law of Christ' is much harder than the 'law of Moses'. The law of Moses says 'do not kill anybody', and 'do not commit adultery'. Many people are clear at that level, but the Law of Christ says 'do not even think about it'. It is much harder to keep the Law of Christ than the law of Moses.

On the other hand, it is much easier in some ways because now we do not need a great number of priests, rituals and special buildings. The apostle John wrote, 'For the law was given through Moses; grace and truth came through Jesus Christ.' Whenever we pray we can enter the holiest place of all unhindered in the name of Jesus.

There is a big difference, too, between the New Covenant and the Old. Under the law given at Pentecost 3,000 died, but with the Spirit given at Pentecost 3,000 lived. I would rather have the Spirit who writes the law on the heart than the old law.

The theme of glory also has a new meaning for Christians. Paul compares the fading glory of Moses with the Spirit's work in the New Covenant. Christians can know the same glory that Moses knew when he came down from the mountain. This glory, however, is not connected with altars, incense and robes but with the Spirit who indwells the believer. This glory increases day by day.

Finally, we must note the way in which the tabernacle speaks so powerfully of how we approach God today. We come first through sacrifice (the altar), justified through Christ, then we need cleansing by the Spirit (the laver). The colours of the tabernacle are significant: purple speaking of royalty, blue of heaven and white of purity. Today we have a High Priest who represents us before God, but one who needs no sacrifice for his own sins. He made the once-and-for-all sacrifice to which all the sacrifices under the Old Covenant point.

There is still to come a future deliverance for Christians equivalent to the Exodus. In Revelation we find that over half the plagues of Pharaoh are going to happen all over again. There is an astonishing correlation between the plagues at the end of history and the plagues which were visited on Pharaoh. Those who remain faithful to Jesus will come through these and be victorious. Chapter 15 of the book of Revelation says that the martyrs, and those who have overcome all the pressures of persecution outside and temptation inside, will sing the song of Moses. In Exodus 15 we have the first song recorded in the Bible, a song composed by Miriam to celebrate the drowning of the Egyptians in the Red Sea. This song will be sung when all this world's troubles are over and we are safe in glory. We will have a double exodus to celebrate – the Exodus from Egypt and the exodus of the cross.

PART III

LEVITICUS

Introduction

Many people who resolve to read the Bible all the way through get stuck in Leviticus. It is easy to understand why. It is a very difficult book to read, for three main reasons.

The first is that it is quite simply a boring book – it is like trying to read the telephone directory. It is so different in content from other books of the Bible, especially the first two, which are full of stories. In these books there is a plot, there is drama, things are moving. When you get into Leviticus there is hardly any narrative at all and, since many regard the Bible as a collection of stories, it is a great disappointment to arrive at a book which has no stories of any kind.

The second reason is that it is so unfamiliar. It is from a different culture as well as having a different content. We are moving away from our present situation by 3,000 years and 2,000 miles. It is a totally different world and we read about things that we find very strange. For example, consider the way they deal with infectious disease in Leviticus. The poor person has to tear their clothes, let their hair grow long and unbrushed, cover the lower part of their face and go around shouting, 'Unclean! Unclean!'. In our society we deal with infectious diseases rather differently! It also includes other weird activities – we do not arrive at church today carrying a little lamb or a pigeon to give to the pastor, who then slits its throat in front of the whole congregation.

The third reason is that it seems to be so irrelevant. What has Leviticus got to say to me living today? At work on a Monday? Deep down we know instinctively that we are not under the law of Moses and, since this book is part of his law, we are not sure what – if anything – it has to do with us.

Context

Let us therefore consider the book with a view to overturning some of the misgivings we may have. Leviticus is one of five books that together make up what is called the Pentateuch (*penta* meaning 'five'). These comprise the law of Moses. The Jews call it the Torah, the 'Books of Instruction', and they read it through once a year. They start on the eighth day of the Feast of Tabernacles, sometime in September/October, and

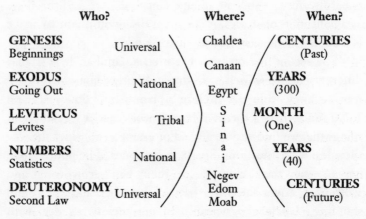

'PENTATEUCH' – 5 books of Moses – 'TORAH' – instruction

	Who?		Where?	When?	
GENESIS Beginnings	Universal		Chaldea	**CENTURIES** (Past)	
			Canaan		
EXODUS Going Out	National		Egypt	**YEARS** (300)	
LEVITICUS Levites		Tribal	S i n a i	**MONTH** (One)	
NUMBERS Statistics	National			**YEARS** (40)	
DEUTERONOMY Second Law	Universal		Negev Edom Moab	**CENTURIES** (Future)	

beginning with Genesis 1, they read it through the year to ish at the next Feast of Tabernacles the following autumn.

The interesting thing about the five books of Moses is that they have a distinctive and memorable shape. Noting this will help us put Leviticus in context. The diagram will make this clear.

ITS PLACE IN THE PENTATEUCH

Genesis is the book of beginnings: it is what the word 'genesis' means and it tells you how everything began, from the creation of our universe to Israel becoming the people of God. Exodus focuses on the Israelites going out from Egypt. Leviticus derives its name from the tribe of Levites, one of the tribes of Israel. The book of Numbers is precisely what it says: a book of statistics (600,000 men came out of Egypt, plus women and children, probably 2.5 million in all). Finally, Deuteronomy (*deutero* means 'second' and *nomus* means 'law') focuses on the second giving of the law (God gave his law twice, once at Sinai and once just before they crossed the Jordan into the Promised Land, so the Ten Commandments come twice – once in Exodus and once in Deuteronomy as a kind of reminder of the law just before they entered the Promised Land).

When we ask who these books are about, we begin to see the shape emerging. Genesis is a universal book – it is about everybody, the human race and the whole universe. Exodus is a national book – it zooms down on one people, the nation of Israel. In Leviticus the focus is even more narrow, on only one tribe out of the whole nation. Once past Leviticus, the focus opens out again and Numbers is about the whole nation once more. Deuteronomy puts Israel against the backcloth of the entire world and we are back to the universal viewpoint.

This shape helps to explain why so many people get stuck in Leviticus. While they are interested in universal things and even national things, they are less concerned when the focus is upon a particular tribe, other than their own.

ITS PLACE IN GEOGRAPHY

Genesis begins with the whole earth, then starts to focus in on the area of the Chaldees where Abraham lived, then on the land of Canaan to which he travelled, and then on Egypt where his descendants ended up. In the land of Egypt they became slaves for 400 years. In Leviticus the focus is once again very narrow, concentrating on just one place: Mount Sinai, where the law and regulations were given. The focus then expands with the journeys through the Negev, Edom and Moab, back into Canaan.

ITS PLACE IN TIME

Genesis covers centuries, all the past history of our earth. Exodus covers years, about 300. Leviticus only covers one month, while Numbers covers 40 years and Deuteronomy looks forward through the centuries to the future history of Israel. Once again we can see the shape of the five books of Moses. Leviticus is the hinge of the whole thing, focusing down to the most important month at the most important place with the most important tribe. The whole of the law of Moses hangs on this.

When the Jews read through the Pentateuch every 12 months, they spend about a fortnight to three weeks reading Leviticus.

Relation to Exodus

Having looked at Leviticus in the context of the Pentateuch, we should also relate it back to Exodus. It is very important to recognize how each book grows out of the previous book if we wish to understand it fully. In the second half of Exodus the tabernacle is built, God's tent in which he lives among his people. If you imagine the camp in Exodus, God's tent would be in the middle and hundreds of other tents all around it – the divine tent and the human tents together. Leviticus is about everything that goes on in God's tent and everything that should go on in the people's tents. So it divides into two halves: God's tent and the people's tents, with the rules and regulations for both.

Furthermore, when dealing with the tabernacle, Exodus talks about God's approach to man, but Leviticus talks about man's approach to God. Exodus is about the deliverance that God brought to his people, but Leviticus is about the dedication of God's people to him. Exodus is about God's grace in setting the people free, but Leviticus begins with thank offerings, explaining how the people can show their gratitude to God for being set free.

We need both books and their complementary messages. This book may not be as exciting as Exodus, but it shows that God expects something from us in return for what he has done for us. Once again we are reminded that we are saved in order to serve. Exodus shows how God saved his people, but Leviticus explains how they are to serve him.

'Be holy'

When we read the Old Testament it can be helpful to imagine that we are Jewish. For a Jewish person the reason for reading Leviticus is clear: it is quite literally a matter of life and death. To the Jews there is only one God and that is the God of Israel. All other so-called gods are figments of human imagination. It was the same for the Israelites in Exodus and Leviticus. Since there was only one God and they were his only people on earth, there was a special relationship between them. On God's side he promised to do many things for them: to be their government; to be their minister of defence and protect them; to be their minister of finance, so there would be no poor among them; to be their minister of health, so that none of the diseases of Egypt would touch them. God would be everything they needed, their King. In return he expected them to live right and to do things right. The biblical word is 'righteous' – 'righteousness' means living right. The key text in the whole of Leviticus is one that is frequently alluded to in the New Testament: 'Be holy for I am holy'.

God expects the people he liberates to be like him and not like those around them. Many of the things which seem puzzling in Leviticus are explained by this fact. It is the key that unlocks the whole book. When God tells them that they must not do something, it is because the people around them are doing it but they are to be different, to be holy because he is holy. If God saves you he expects you to be like him; he expects you to live his way and to be holy as he is holy.

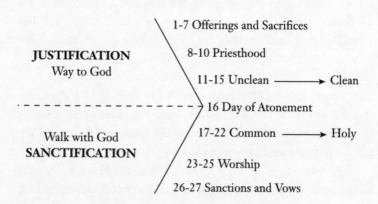

JUSTIFICATION
Way to God

1-7 Offerings and Sacrifices

8-10 Priesthood

11-15 Unclean ⟶ Clean

16 Day of Atonement

17-22 Common ⟶ Holy

23-25 Worship

26-27 Sanctions and Vows

Walk with God
SANCTIFICATION

The shape of the book

We have noted already that the book is in two halves. It builds up to a climax and then flows out from the climax. It is also like a multi-layered sandwich. The chart shows that the first section corresponds to the last, the second to the second last, and the third to the third last, leaving one right in the middle. There are clear correspondences between these sections, beautifully put together and worked out.

Remember that God is responsible for this pattern, not Moses. In fact, there are more words of God in the book of Leviticus than in any other book in the Bible! About 90 per cent of Leviticus is the direct speech of God – 'The LORD said to Moses...' There is no other book in the Bible that has so much of God's direct speech, so if you want to read God's Word this is a good book to start with. You will be reading the actual words of God.

The offerings and sacrifices of the first seven chapters are backed up by the sanctions and vows of the people in the last section. The details about the priesthood correspond to the details about the worship that they are to lead.

The climax of the book is the Day of Atonement, the day on which two animals were used to symbolize the sins of the people. They sacrificed one animal, a sheep, inside the camp. One after another they then laid their hands on the other animal, a goat, and confessed their sins. They pushed the goat out of the camp into the wilderness, where it would die with all their sins loaded on it. It was called the 'scapegoat', a word we still have in common use today.

The two sections of the book pivot around the Day of Atonement. The first half describes our way to God – what we call **justification** – and the second half describes our walk with God – what is known as **sanctification**.

Offerings and worship

Let us look first at the opening seven chapters, which deal with the rules for offerings. There are five offerings, of two different types.

Gratitude offerings

The first three offerings were the right way to say 'thank you' to God for blessing. They were not offerings for sin but offerings of gratitude. If we feel grateful to God he wants us to say 'thank you'.

For the **burnt offering**, an animal was brought, slaughtered and then burnt so that God could smell it. The sacrifice was said to be a sweet-smelling savour to him.

In a burnt offering the whole thing was burnt, but for a **meal offering** some was kept back so that the worshipper could have a meal with God. Part of the offering would be given to God and part would be eaten by the person making the offering.

The third gratitude offering was a **peace offering**, in which all the fat was burned.

Guilt offerings

The other two offerings were not to express gratitude but to deal with guilt. There was the **sin offering** and the **trespass offering** and these did two things.

First, they made atonement for sin. They offered God compensation for what the person had done wrong. The word 'atonement' does not mean 'at-one-ment' – that is a modern idea. It actually means 'compensation', so if you atone for something, you offer something as compensation. Both the sin offering and trespass offering are compensation offerings to God involving blood: as a compensation for the bad life the offerer has lived, they offer to God a good life that has not sinned.

Second, they only work for unintentional sins; they do not work for deliberate sins. In other words, nobody is perfect, we all make mistakes, we all fall into sin unintentionally. Even though we did not intend to do wrong, we did it. God provided offerings for unintentional sin, but there is no offering on this list for deliberate sin.

This is an important point which is picked up in the New Testament. The New Testament distinguishes between accidental and deliberate, wilful sin in Christians. Like the Old Testament, it says that if we deliberately sin after being forgiven, there is no more sacrifice for sin. Deliberate sin in those who have been forgiven is very serious, which is why Jesus said to the woman caught in adultery, 'Go and sin no more'. For accidental sin, however, there is full provision, because God knows we are weak, knows we fall, and knows we do not always intend to do what we do. As Paul says in Romans: 'The evil I would not, that I do.' This distinction between deliberate sin and accidental sin in God's people runs right through the New Testament as it does through the Old.

Worship calendar

As well as bringing offerings to God, the Jews had a calendar of worship to observe. There is no corresponding Christian calendar in the New Testament, no instructions about observing Christmas or Easter, but for the Jewish people a calendar was a vital part of their walk with God. They were being treated as children: adults do not need a calendar but children do, to remind them of things they would otherwise forget. Various types of feast are mentioned in Leviticus, and all had to be kept.

ANNUAL FEASTS

The calendar began in the first month of the year, which is roughly our March/April, with **Passover**, the Feast of Unleavened Bread. This took place on the fifteenth day of the first month, to remember how God brought the Israelites out of slavery in Egypt. On the day before the Passover began, a lamb had to be killed at 3.00 p.m.

Three days later (i.e. three days after the slaughter of the lamb) they had to offer the **Firstfruits** of the harvest to God. It is not difficult to discern the similarities in pattern with Jesus' death and resurrection.

Fifty days after that they were to hold the **Feast of Pentecost** (*pente* meaning '50'), or the Feast of Weeks. This was the day that the law was given on Sinai. They were to remember this and give thanks for it. When the law was given at Sinai on the very first Pentecost, 3,000 people were put to death because of their sin. Centuries later, when the Spirit was given at Pentecost, 3,000 were saved.

Next come the feasts towards the end of the year (the 'seventh month', or our September/October). At the **Feast of Trumpets**, the *shofar*, the old ram's horn, was blown. This signalled a whole new round of feasts.

Then came the **Day of Atonement**, the crucial day when the scapegoat was pushed out of the camp with all the sins of the people on its back.

The **Feast of Tabernacles** (also known as the Feast of Succoth) came after that, lasting eight days. For this feast they moved out of their houses and lived in shelters. They had to be able to see the stars through the roof to remind them of their 40 years of foolish wandering in the wilderness when they could have reached the Promised Land in just 11 days.

All these feasts will be fulfilled in a Christian way. The first three have already been fulfilled in the first coming of Jesus.

The second three will be fulfilled at his second coming. We cannot know the year that Jesus will return, but we do know that it will be around September/October, because he always does things on time. Indeed, this was the time when he was born: the evidence in Luke's Gospel points to the seventh month of the year, which corresponds to the Feast of Tabernacles. This is when the Jews expect the Messiah. Every time a trumpet is mentioned in the New Testament it is to announce his coming. When that happens, the last three feasts will be fulfilled, and on that Day of Atonement redemption will come to the whole nation of Israel.

WEEKLY HOLY DAY

In addition to the annual festivals, there was also to be a weekly rest, a particular blessing for people who had been slaves in Egypt. There is no trace of the **Sabbath** in the Bible before Moses. Both Adam and Abraham, for example, had no Sabbath day: they worked seven days a week. Moses introduced this weekly day of rest. It was not to be a holiday or a family day but a day for God, a holy day, and this was part of their calendar.

JUBILEE

But there were not only annual and weekly festivals – there was also to be a festival every 50 years, known as the **Jubilee**. Every 50 years everybody's bank balance was levelled up, and all the property reverted to the family who originally owned it. So the leases would get cheaper the closer you came to the fiftieth year. Slaves were also set free in the jubilee year. Thus people looked forward to the jubilee, known also as 'the acceptable year of the Lord'. It was good news for the poor because they would be rich again, and it was a time when captives would be set at liberty.

Jesus proclaimed in Nazareth: 'The Spirit of the Lord is on me ... to preach good news to the poor ... to proclaim freedom for the prisoners ... to proclaim the year of the Lord's favour.' In other words, Jesus began the real jubilee to which every one of these people had been looking forward. Once again the Old Testament is needed to understand the New.

Rules for living

Clean and unclean

A crucial area to understand in Leviticus concerns the distinctions between holy and common, clean and unclean. Most

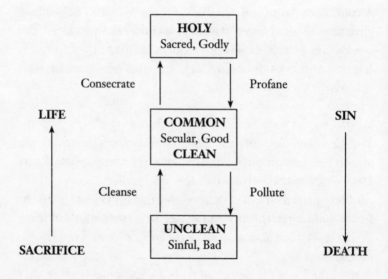

people think in terms of good and bad, but the Bible works with three categories, as the chart shows.*

There are two processes going on. The first process is when sacred, godly, holy things are profaned and become common. You can spoil a holy thing by making it common. When the Bible Society sent Bibles to Romania, the communist government allowed the pages to be used in toilet rolls. It sparked a revolution started by Christians who were scandalized by this action. What had happened in that situation according to the teaching of Leviticus? In using the Bible for such a mundane though necessary purpose, a holy thing had been made common. The second process is when a common, clean thing is made unclean and sinful.

The three words *sacred*, *secular* and *sinful* correspond roughly to these divisions of *holy*, *clean and common*, and *unclean*. Just as there is a process of profaning the holy to make it common, and polluting the common and clean to make it unclean, so there is a process of redeeming this situation. You can cleanse the unclean and make it clean, then you can consecrate it and it becomes holy.

What is holy and what is unclean must never come into contact. They must be kept rigidly apart. Things holy and things unclean have nothing in common. If there is a mixture of unclean and clean it will make both unclean. Similarly, if you mix holy and common things, that makes them all common – it does not make them all holy.

Hence the downward process shown on the chart leads to death, quite literally, whereas the upward process leads to life –

* For the illuminating distinction between holy, clean and unclean, I am indebted to G. J. Wenham, in his *New International Commentary on Leviticus* (Wm. B Eerdmans, Grand Rapids, Michigan, 1979).

but this involves sacrifice. Only by sacrifice can you cleanse what is unclean and bring it to life.

This has ramifications for our view of life. According to the Bible our work can be consecrated to God. Work can be any of these three things, holy, clean or unclean. There are some jobs that are illegal and immoral, which are therefore unclean. A Christian should not be in them. There are other jobs that are clean, but common. But you can consecrate your work and do it for the Lord, and then it ceases to be common – it becomes a holy vocation in the Lord. So it is possible for a printer to be doing holy work, just as it is possible for a missionary to do only common work. Your money can be unclean if it is spent on bad things, clean if it is spent on good things, or holy if it is consecrated to the Lord. Sex, too, can be any one of these three things.

Plenty of people are living decent, common, clean lives, but they are not holy people. God does not want us just to be living good lives: he wants us to be living holy lives. This is the emphasis in Leviticus.

Those outside the Church may claim that they can live lives as good as the lives of those within it, but they are not the holy people God is looking for.

Holy living

Living holy lives involves all kinds of very practical things.

- The **health** of the body is just as important to holiness as the health of the spirit. What we do with our bodies does matter if we want to be holy to the Lord. Leviticus has instructions about haircuts, tattoos and men wearing earrings, as well as regulations on male and female bodily discharges and childbirth.

- There are a lot of regulations concerning **food** here, clean and unclean food especially.
- There is teaching in Leviticus about not getting involved in **occultism** or with spiritualist mediums.
- Instructions are given on the action to be taken when there is **dry rot** in the house. The house is to be torn down in love for your neighbour.
- There is teaching concerning **clothing**. There is to be no mixed material.
- **Social life** is covered: holiness means paying special attention to the poor, the deaf, the blind, and the aged. If you are a holy youth you will stand up when an older person comes into the room.
- **Sex** is also dealt with. Leviticus has things to say on incest, buggery and homosexuality.

If you ask what is a holy life, Leviticus says it is how you live from Monday to Saturday and not just what you do on Sunday. God is looking not just for clean people, but for holy people. That is a big difference and until you become a Christian you never even think of becoming holy; you just think of being good – and that is not good enough.

Rules and regulations

We need to be clear about our understanding of the law of Moses. It is called the 'law', not the 'laws', because it all hangs together. Holiness means wholeness, and all these rules and regulations fit together and form one whole. If you break any of them you have broken them all. (In the chapter on Exodus I likened the breaking of one of the Commandments to breaking a necklace, which causes all the beads to scatter.) This fact cuts across most people's view of the Ten Commandments. It is generally thought that if we can keep a high percentage of the laws we are doing well! This is not enough.

REASONS

God did not give reasons for all his rules. He did not tell us why we should not wear clothing of mixed materials, for example, or why we should not crossbreed animals or sow mixed seed. We can perhaps see a reason, however, in the fact that God is a God of purity – so he does not like mixed material for clothes, or mixed seed or mixed breeding. Although he does not always give the reasons for a prohibition, in some cases we can make an informed guess. The reason in some cases is undoubtedly hygiene. Some of the regulations about toilets are obvious, for example: there are hygienic reasons behind what God told them to do. Also it may be that some of the food forbidden as 'unclean' was also prohibited because of health concerns. Pig's flesh, for instance, was peculiarly liable to disease in that climate.

Where there are no reasons given, the people were simply to obey because they trusted that the law-giver knew why he had commanded it. In the same way, there are times in the family home when children need to be told that they are to do something 'because Daddy says so'. Sometimes to give the reason would be inappropriate, or it would be impossible to explain.

With many of the laws God is saying: Do you trust me? Do you believe that if I tell you not to do something I have a very good reason for that?

Too often we are only prepared to do something after we are convinced that it is for our good. We want to be God. Just like Adam and Eve, who took the fruit of the tree of the knowledge of good and evil, we want to decide, to experience and to settle it for ourselves. But God has no obligation to explain himself to us.

Sanctions

God may not give reasons, but he does give sanctions. There is a call for obedience, but the *cost of disobedience* is also spelt out. And the punishments are pretty severe. In Leviticus 26, therefore, a whole collection of positive reasons for being obedient is laid out, but by the same token there is also a curse on those who disobey. If a Jew reads the book of Leviticus, he finds that a number of things could happen if he disobeys God's law.

He could lose his home, he could lose his citizenship and he could lose his life. There are 15 sins mentioned in Leviticus for which capital punishment is the consequence. Maybe now we can see why understanding this book was so critical – it is literally a matter of life and death.

Furthermore, Leviticus makes clear that the nation as a whole can lose two things. They could lose their freedom, being invaded by enemies from outside (we see this in the book of Judges). Or they could lose their land, being driven out and made slaves somewhere else. In time, both these things happened to the nation of Israel. These were not empty promises and threats. There are rewards for trusting and obeying God, but there are also punishments for those who distrust and disobey him.

HAPPINESS AND HOLINESS

What God is actually saying through this combination of rewards and punishments is that the only way to be really happy is to be really holy. Happiness and holiness belong together and the lack of holiness brings unhappiness. Most people get it the wrong way round. God's will for us is that we be holy in this world and happy in the next, but many want to be happy in this world and holy later.

God is willing to let things happen to us which may be painful, but which will make us more holy as a result. Our character tends to make more progress in the tough times than the good.

Reading Leviticus as Christians

What has this book to say to us, living as Christians in the modern world? Do we have to get rid of all mixed-fibre clothing? If we get dry rot in the house, do we have to burn it down?

One principle we can use as a guide is found in Paul's second letter to Timothy. Paul writes: 'From infancy you have known the holy Scriptures, which are able to make you wise for salvation through faith in Christ Jesus. All Scripture is God-breathed and is useful for teaching, rebuking, correcting and training in righteousness, so that the man of God may be thoroughly equipped for every good work'.

Paul is talking to Timothy about the Old Testament. The New Testament did not exist when he wrote this, so 'the Scriptures' referred to must be the Old Testament. When Jesus said, 'Search the Scriptures, for they bear witness to me,' he meant the Old Testament. We can learn about two things from the Old Testament: salvation and righteousness. This goes for Leviticus as well. It, too, can help us understand how to be saved, and it will open our eyes to right living. Those two purposes just shine out.

Leviticus in the New Testament

It is always very illuminating to see what the New Testament does with an Old Testament book. As somebody said: 'The Old is in the New revealed, the New is in the Old concealed.' The two belong together and each Testament outlines the other.

There are a number of direct quotations from Leviticus in the New Testament, but two in particular come very frequently:

'Be holy, for I am holy' and 'You shall love your neighbour as yourself.' There are many other passages where parts of Leviticus are clearly in mind, and in particular we cannot understand the letter to the Hebrews unless we read Leviticus. These two belong to each other. Hebrews could not have been written unless Leviticus had been written first.

There are over 90 references to Leviticus in the New Testament, so it is a very important book for Christians to get to grips with.

THE FULFILMENT OF THE LAW

What, then, are we to make of the law of Moses today, remembering that there are not just 10 laws but 613 in total? We may have a hunch that we are not tied to them all, but how many *are* we tied to? For example, some churches teach their members to tithe. Others have strict rules about the Sabbath, even if for them the Sabbath is Sunday, not Saturday as observed by the Jews? Every Christian has to come to terms with this difficulty. It is complicated by the fact that Jesus said, 'I have not come to destroy the law, but to fulfil it.'

We must therefore ask how each law is fulfilled. It is obvious that some are fulfilled in Christ and finished with. That is why you do not have to take a pigeon or a lamb to church when you go to worship next Sunday. The laws about blood sacrifices have been fulfilled.

In a similar way the Sabbath law is fulfilled for us every day of the week when we cease to do our own works and do God's instead, thus entering into the rest that remains for the people of God. We are still free to keep one day special if we wish, but we are also free to regard every day alike. So we cannot even impose Sunday observance on other believers, never mind unbelievers, for we are all free in Christ.

It is very important to realize exactly what the fulfilment of each law is. Of the Ten Commandments, nine are repeated in the New Testament in exactly the same way, e.g. you shall not steal, you shall not commit adultery. The Sabbath one is not, being fulfilled in a very different way.

Other laws of Moses are fulfilled in different ways. One law in Deuteronomy says, for example, that when you are using an ox to thresh the corn, walking round and round, its hooves breaking the wheat from the chaff, you must not put a muzzle on it because it has every right to eat what it is preparing for others. This is fulfilled in the New Covenant. Paul quotes that law and gives it a completely different fulfilment, explaining that in the same way those who live for the gospel have a right to expect financial support from others. It is necessary to look at each law and see how it is fulfilled in the New Testament and given a deeper meaning.

There are, however, four crucial things that we learn from the book of Leviticus which are *unchanged* in the New Testament.

1. THE HOLINESS OF GOD

There is no book in the Bible which is stronger on the holiness of God than Leviticus and it is something we forget at our peril, especially in an age when people ask the question: 'How can a God of love send anyone to hell?' We know through Jesus that God is a God of love, and Jesus also spoke openly about hell. We cannot pick and choose: if Jesus told the truth about God being a God of love, we must also accept that he spoke the truth about hell.

Actually, God's understanding of love is a little different from ours. Ours is sentimental love, his is holy love. His love is so great that he hates evil. Very few of us love enough to hate evil. We learn about the holiness of God from the book of

Leviticus. We learn to love God with reverence, with holy fear. Hebrews says, 'Let us worship God with reverence and awe, for our God is a consuming fire.' This is a sentiment the writer got straight out of Leviticus. It is vital for Christians today to read Leviticus, in order to keep hold of this sense of God's holiness.

2. THE SINFULNESS OF MAN

Leviticus strongly underlines the sinfulness of man as well as the holiness of God. It is so realistic and down to earth. Here is human nature, capable of bestiality, incest, superstitions, and many other things which are an abomination to God. 'Abomination' means something that makes you want to be physically sick because you are so disgusted. The Hebrew word for it is a very, very strong expression; the English translations – abomination, loathsome, vile, revolting – are all just poor substitutes.

The Bible is about God's emotions. God's emotional reaction to sin comes because he is holy. The sinfulness of man is not just in polluting clean things, but also in profaning holy things. Common swearing is the profaning of holy words. There are only two sacred relationships in our lives – that between us and God, and that between man and woman. Ninety per cent of swearwords come from one of these two relationships. Mankind profanes holy things and pollutes clean things. We live in a world that is doing both, and the sinfulness of man is not only in making clean things dirty, but in making holy things common and in treating things as common when they are not.

3. THE FULLNESS OF CHRIST

Leviticus points towards the fullness of Christ and his sacrifice, once for all. God has provided a way of cleansing the sin from mankind. His problem is how to reconcile justice and mercy. Should he deal with this sin in justice and punish us, or should he deal with it in mercy and forgive us? Since God is both just and merciful, he must find a way of being just and merciful at the same time. It is impossible for us to find a way, but it has been possible for him – by the substitution of an innocent life for a guilty life. Only when that happens are both justice and mercy satisfied. The sacrificial laws of Leviticus begin to show us how that can happen.

There are particular words associated with this process which occur many times. 'Atonement' and 'blood' are frequently mentioned, because in the blood is the life. If a person's blood is taken away, their life is taken away. 'Offerings' are also frequently mentioned. The burnt offering speaks of the total *surrender* that is needed. The meal offering speaks of our *service*. The peace offering tells us of the *serenity* we can have with God. These are the three things that should characterize a grateful life, a life that has been saved.

Yet we note too God's side of the equation, his *sacrifice*. The only sacrifices we now have to bring to the Lord are the sacrifices of praise and thanksgiving, and these should be properly prepared and brought before him. But the sacrifices in Leviticus also speak of the sacrifice that Jesus made. The sin offering tells us about the *substitution* of an innocent life for the guilty, and the trespass offering brings home to us that this sacrifice *satisfies* divine justice, that there is some law that is being met by it. It all looks straight forward to the New Testament.

4. GODLINESS OF LIFE

Leviticus tells us to be holy in every part of our lives, even down to our toilet arrangements! Holiness is wholeness, which is why we can read of the incredible detail God goes into as he applies his holiness to every part of his people's lives. It tells you that a godly life is godly through and through or it is not godly at all.

It is important to note, however, that there are two major shifts between the holiness of the Old Covenant and the holiness of the New. In Leviticus there is the triple division between holy, clean and unclean. This still applies in the New Testament, but there are two major alterations to it.

First, holiness is moved from material things to moral things. The children of Israel *were* children and they had to be taught as children. They had to learn the difference between clean and unclean in matters of food, for example. Christians have no such rules, however. It took a vision to teach this to the apostle Peter. Jesus said that it is not what goes into your mouth that makes you unclean now, but what comes *out* of your mouth. Being clean or unclean is no longer a matter of clothes and food, but of clean and unclean morality. It has shifted from the material to the moral. Now we do not have all those regulations about clothes and food, but we do have a lot of teaching about how to be holy in moral questions.

Second, the rewards and punishments are shifted from this life to the next. In this world holy people may well suffer and not be rewarded, but the shift has happened because in the New Testament we have a longer-term view. This life is not the only one there is – it is only the preparation for a much longer existence elsewhere. So in the New Testament we read 'great is your reward in heaven', not on earth.

Given these two major shifts, Leviticus is a most profitable book for Christians to read. Above all, it gives us insight into those four vital things: the holiness of God, the sinfulness of man, the fullness of Christ, and godliness of life.

PART IV

NUMBERS

Introduction

Numbers is not a well-known book, neither is it widely quoted. Perhaps only two verses are well known. Samuel Morse quoted one of these after he sent the first telegraph message in Morse code to Washington DC on 24 May 1844. He expressed his amazement at what had happened with the verse, 'What hath God wrought?' (translated in the NIV as 'See what God has done.') The discovery of electronic communication was attributed to the God who had given the power.

The second verse is known by most people: 'Be sure your sin will find you out'. This was originally said by Moses as a warning to the people when he was telling them that they must cross the Jordan and fight their enemies.

Neither verse is generally known to come from Numbers. Very few people are able to quote verses from the book and I have found that few know what any one chapter contains. We need to remedy this situation, as Numbers is another very important part of the Bible.

'Numbers' is a strange title for a book. In the Hebrew the title is taken from the first words of the scroll, 'The LORD said'. When the Hebrew Scriptures were translated into Greek, the translators gave it a new title, *Arithmoi* (from which we get the word 'arithmetic'). The Latin (Vulgate) version translated this as *numeri*. So in English we know it as 'Numbers'.

It begins and ends with two censuses. The first was taken when Israel left Sinai one month after the tabernacle had been erected. The total number of people counted was 603,550. The second was taken when they arrived at Moab prior to entering the land of Canaan almost 40 years later. The number of people had dropped by 1,820 to 601,730 – not a very great difference. These were male censuses used for military conscription.

The book of Numbers tells us that there is nothing wrong with counting. King David was punished by God for counting his men, but this was because he was motivated by pride. Other parts of the Bible include examples of counting and taking stock – we are told, for example, that 3,000 were added to the Church at Pentecost. Jesus encouraged his followers to count the cost of following him by reflecting on how the leader of an army might evaluate his chances according to the relative strength of his army.

Three things can be said about the figures given in Numbers.

1. What a large number!

Many Bible commentators question the size of the numbers. The figures actually represent the military conscription – the men over 20 years old who were able to fight. We have seen already in our studies of Exodus that there were over 2 million people in total, so the 'large' number of 603,550 is actually a fraction of the whole population. There are a number of points to consider which indicate that the numbers given are, in fact, feasible and reasonable.

- In 2 Samuel we are told that David's army was 1,300,000, so a figure of around 600,000 is small in comparison.
- The number is also small in comparison to the Canaanites. The Israelites would need to be of a certain strength in order to fight battles (remembering, nevertheless, that God was on their side).
- Those who argue that it is impossible for the 70 families who came to Egypt to produce so many forget that the people were in Egypt for 400 years. If each generation had four children (a small figure for those times), the figure is possible.
- Some say it is too great a number to fit into the wilderness of Sinai. It is feasible, however: there was enough space. If they travelled five abreast, the column would be 110 miles long and it would take 10 days to pass!
- Some say these numbers mean that there were too many people to be fed successfully in the wilderness. That would certainly have been the case, but for God's supernatural provision.

2. What a similar number!

Given the magnitudes involved, a difference of 1,820 between the first and second censuses represents a very small percentage change. The tribe of Simeon had lost 37,100 and Manasseh had gained 20,500, but most remained about the same. Since numerical growth indicates God's blessing, we can note from the outset that this was not a period when God was pleased with his people. Considering the hostile environment and the length of time, however, maintaining such numbers was remarkable.

3. What a different number!

There were over 38 years between the two censuses, so a whole generation perished in the wilderness. (It was rare for men to reach 60; Moses was an exception to live until 120.) So although the number was similar, the people were not. Only Joshua and Caleb (2 out of 2 million) survived from those who left Egypt to enter the Promised Land. In some ways this is the biggest tragedy in the whole Bible. Numbers is a very *sad* book. Two-thirds of the book need never have been written. It should have taken 11 days to travel from Egypt to the Promised Land, but it actually took them 13,780 days! Only two of those who set out actually reached their home. The rest were stuck in an aimless existence, 'killing time' until God's judgement was complete. Over time they all died in the wilderness, and a new generation took up the journey.

Most lessons we learn from Numbers are negative. This is how *not* to be the people of God! Paul tells us how we should view it in 1 Corinthians 10: 'Now these things occurred as examples to keep us from setting our hearts on evil things as they did ... These things happened to them as examples and were written down as warnings for us, on whom the fulfilment of the ages has come.' Numbers is full of bad 'examples'.

Context

What, then, is the context for this book? The journey from Mount Sinai to Kadesh Barnea (the last oasis in the Negev Desert) and the beginning of the Promised Land of Canaan takes 11 days on foot. The route the Israelites took was to turn away from Kadesh and go across the Rift Valley, to the mountains of Edom. They finished up in Moab on the wrong side of the River Jordan. It took 38 years and a few months, not because it was a particularly difficult piece of country but because God only moved a little at a time. He stayed a very long time in each place and told them he would wait until every man among them was dead, except Joshua and Caleb.

What happened to bring God's judgement down on the people? At Kadesh the people refused to enter the land when God told them to. Today many Christians have been brought out of sin but have not enjoyed the blessing that God has set out for them. They too end up in a miserable wilderness.

Two-thirds of the book of Numbers is about this protracted journey. The Bible is a very honest book, telling us about failures and vices as well as great successes and virtues. When Paul told the Corinthians that Numbers was written down as an example and a warning to us, he meant this as a clear statement of the book's purpose. It may not be a popular book, but if you do not study history you are condemned to repeat it.

Even Moses was not permitted to go into the Promised Land, although he did enter it centuries later when he talked with Jesus. He too failed miserably at one crucial point, as we shall see.

Content and structure

Another of the five books of Moses, Numbers is a mixture of legislation and narrative. The author of the laws is not Moses but God. We are told 80 times in this book, 'God said to Moses...' God gives to Moses general laws and legislation, as well as regulations governing rituals and religious ceremony.

As for the narrative in the book, we are told that Moses kept a journal of their travels at the Lord's command. He also kept another book called 'the book of the Wars of the LORD', recording accounts of the battles. Numbers was written by Moses using these records, yet Moses himself is referred to in the third person

The mixture of narrative and legislation makes it seem rather like Exodus, but whereas in Exodus the first half is narrative and the second half law, in Numbers it is all mixed up. It is therefore much harder to find a connecting thread.

A pattern emerges more easily when we consider the narrative and legislation in context. The structure of the book is *chronological* rather than topical. We can see this best by putting the content of Numbers alongside that of Exodus, Leviticus and Deuteronomy.

Chronological context	Content	Duration
Exodus 1–18 *Egypt to Sinai*	Narrative	50 days
Exodus 19–40 *at Sinai*	Legislation	?
Leviticus 1–27 *at Sinai*	Legislation	30 days
Numbers 1:1–10:10 *at Sinai*	Legislation	19 days
Numbers 10:11–12:16		
Sinai to Kadesh	Narrative	11 days
Numbers 13:1–20:21 *Kadesh*	Legislation	?
Numbers 20:22–21:35		
Kadesh to Moab	Narrative	38 years
Numbers 22:1–36:13 *Moab*	Legislation	3 months, 10 days
Deuteronomy 1–34 *Moab*	Legislation	5 months

It is fascinating to note that all the laws were given to the Israelites while they were camped. The stories of their travels show how they broke those laws. While they were camped and stationary God told them what they *should* do, but while they were moving we hear the story of what they *did* do. They would learn lessons both ways, through the teaching from Moses and through the experience of journeying (rather as Jesus taught his disciples both in 'messages', such as the Sermon on the Mount, and as they travelled 'along the way').

The chart given above is like a multi-layered sandwich. Thus in Exodus 1–11 the Israelites are stuck in Egypt, then in Chapters 12–18 they move to Sinai. All this is narrative. However, in Exodus 19–40, Leviticus 1–27 and Numbers 1–10 they are still at Sinai. These three consecutive sections are full of legislation.

In Numbers 10–12 they move again, from Sinai to Kadesh, a journey of 11 days. The stay in Kadesh covers the crisis when the people rebel. God speaks to them at Kadesh from Chapters 13 to 20, again with legislation.

Numbers 20–21 covers the journey from Kadesh to Moab, the whole journey of 38 years covering just two chapters. Numbers 22–36 covers what God said to the Israelites while they waited to go into the Promised Land. The whole of Deuteronomy 1–34 belongs to that same, stationary time period.

Numbers has a lot of movement in it, Deuteronomy has none, and Exodus has movement in just the first half.

Legislation

As noted above, we are told on 80 occasions in Numbers that God spoke to Moses 'face to face'. This was unique: others would receive God's Word through visions when they were awake or dreams when they were asleep. The people would consult the priests' *urim* (the equivalent of 'drawing lots') when they wished to discern God's mind on a situation.

Moses first met with God on Mount Sinai, some distance from the rest of Israel, but now that the tabernacle was constructed God was dwelling with the people. The big danger now that God was 'with them', however, was that they might become overfamiliar, lose their sense of awe and respect, and forget his holiness. The laws in Numbers are not moral or social laws, but laws given to prevent the people from losing their reverence for God. The laws can be classified under three headings: carefulness, cleanliness and costliness.

1. Carefulness

WHEN CAMPED

They had to be very careful to camp in the right place (Chapter 2). Each tribe was allotted a specific place in relation to the other tribes and the tabernacle in the centre. The camp looked like a 'hollow rectangle' from above (see the chart below). The only other nation known to camp in this manner were the Egyptians – this was the preferred arrangement of Rameses II (the Pharaoh who may have been on the throne at the time).

The tabernacle in the centre was surrounded by a fence and there was only one entrance. Two people camped outside the entrance – Moses and Aaron. The Levites camped around the other three sides, and three of their clans had special responsibility – Merari, Gershon and Kohath. No one else could even touch the fence and there were orders to kill anyone who approached. God was holy and could not be approached lightly.

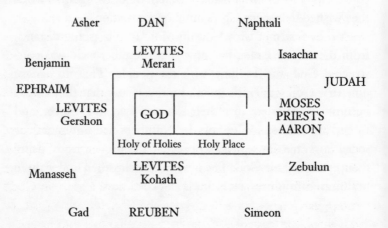

The other tribes were arranged around the tabernacle, each tribe with its own specific, allotted place in relation to God's tent and the entrance to it. The most important place was right in front of the entrance, and this was occupied by the tribe of Judah. It was from the tribe of Judah that Jesus would later come.

WHEN TREKKING

When the camp set out on a journey, everyone moved according to a fascinating pattern. There were specific instructions for the dismantling and transporting of the tabernacle. The priests would wrap up the holy furniture, then the Levites would pick it up. Everyone knew who had to carry which piece of furniture from the tabernacle, who had to carry the curtains, and what order they had to be carried in. Some tribes had to leave before the tabernacle pieces were carried. When the other tribes moved they 'unpeeled' like an orange. They marched in the same order every time, so that when they got to the next camp it was simple for each tribe to find their place and put their tents up. The whole thing is carefully detailed. The silver trumpets would sound to announce the departure from the camp, and the tribe of Judah would lead the procession with praise

They always knew when it was time to move because the pillar of cloud (or fire at night) above the tabernacle would move on. The picture is clear: when God moves, his people move.

Why is God so fussy about all these details? Not only was it a very efficient way to move such a vast quantity of people, but it was also a very efficient way of camping. He was saying, 'Be careful!' A careless attitude does not have a place in God's camp: carelessness is a dangerous thing. A modern word for this would be 'casualness', the 'any old thing will do for God' attitude.

In these detailed directions God is telling his people to be careful, for he is in the camp with them. He also outlines other areas where they would need to be careful. There are some sins mentioned in Numbers which are sins of 'carelessness'. Carelessness on the Sabbath was punishable by death. They were to have tassels on their clothes to remind them to pray. Vows had to be taken very seriously. If a vow was made to God it must be kept. (In Judges we have the story of a man who vowed to sacrifice to God the first living thing that he met when he came out, and he met his daughter!) If a wife makes a vow to God, then her husband has 24 hours to agree or disagree with it.

2. Cleanliness

As well as being carefully arranged, the camp had to be spotlessly clean, for these were 'God's people'. Even such things as the sewage arrangements were carefully detailed. They were told to take a spade when emptying their bowels so that they could keep the camp clean for the Lord. He was not just concerned with germs. God was interested in a 'clean' camp because he is a 'clean' God. The principle still holds today. A dirty, uncared-for church building is an insult to God.

Not only was the *camp* to be clean, we are also told of the cleansing of the *people* before they left Sinai.

There are further details of purification rites in Chapter 19. Death is an unclean thing. God is a God of life, so there was to be no taint of death in the camp. There was even a 'jealousy test' for adulterous wives. Even if there were no witnesses, God sees what happens and will punish the evildoer. This is *his* camp.

The expression 'cleanliness is next to Godliness' has some considerable support from the book of Numbers!

3. Costliness

SACRIFICES AND OFFERINGS

It is costly for a sinful person to live close to a holy God. Sacrifices were offered on behalf of the people on a daily, weekly and monthly basis. There were literally hundreds. Each sacrifice had to be costly – only the best animals were offered.

The daily sacrifice, weekly sacrifice and a special monthly sacrifice made it clear it was a costly matter to receive forgiveness from God. Blood had to be shed.

PRIESTHOOD

Furthermore, the priesthood had to be supported by means of offerings. The Levites were consecrated for service before they left Sinai. Some 8,580 served (out of the 22,000 in the tribe) and both priests and Levites were dependent on the other tribes for their financial support.

The upkeep of the priesthood, plus the regular sacrifices, therefore made up a considerable 'cost' to the people.

This teaches us that we still need to be very careful today about how we approach God. I may not need to bring a ram, pigeon or dove to be sacrificed when I come to God, but that does not mean I do not have to bring a sacrifice at all. There is as much sacrifice in the New Testament as in the Old. We read of the sacrifice of *praise* and the sacrifice of *thanksgiving*, for example. We need to ask ourselves whether we do make sacrifices to God. We too should *prepare* for worship.

Numbers also tells us about the Nazirite vow, a voluntary vow of dedication and devotion to God, although not part of the priesthood. The Nazirites vowed not cut their hair, not to touch alcohol (both were contrary to the social custom of the day) and not to touch a dead body. Some of these vows were temporary, others were for life. Samuel and Samson are the best-known Nazirites in Scripture. By the time of Amos the practice was ridiculed.

WHAT CAN WE LEARN FROM THIS?

Today there is a tendency towards an anti-ritual, casual approach to worship, forgetting that God is exactly the same today as he was then. We too are to approach him with awe and dignity. Hebrews reminds us that he is a consuming fire.

In the New Testament we read of how those gathered for worship may bring a song, a word, a prophecy, a tongue, an interpretation. This is the New Testament equivalent of preparing, approaching God in the right frame of mind.

Numbers also reminds us that we must worship God according to *his* taste and not ours. Modern worship tends to focus on the preferences of individuals, whether this be in favour of hymns or choruses, for example. We can forget that our preferences are quite irrelevant compared to the importance of making sure that our worship matches what God wants.

Our sacrifices of praise and giving are also mentioned in the New Testament: 'They [your gifts] are a fragrant offering, an acceptable sacrifice, pleasing to God.' In Leviticus and Numbers God loved the smell of roast lamb. In the same way, our sacrifice of praise can also be pleasing to God today.

Narrative

In turning to the narrative parts of Numbers, we move from the divine word to human deeds – from what the people *should* do to what they *did* do. It is a sad and sordid story. The wilderness becomes a testing ground for them. They are out of Egypt but not in the Promised Land, and this limbo existence is very hard for them to endure.

We need to remember that the people are now in a covenant relationship with God. He has bound himself to them. He will bless their obedience and punish their disobedience. The same acts of sin are committed in Exodus 16–19 as in Numbers 10–14, but only in Numbers is the law violated, so only in Numbers do the sanctions apply.

God's law can help you see what is right (and wrong), but it cannot help you *do* what is right. The law did not change their behaviour: it brought guilt, condemnation and punishment. This is why the law given on the first Pentecost day was inadequate and later needed the Spirit to be given on that same day. Without supernatural help we would never be able to keep the law.

Leaders

We will look first at the leaders of the nation and see how they tried and failed to live up to the law. They are all from one family, two brothers and a sister – Moses, Aaron and Miriam (an alternative version of the name Mary). We are told their good points and their strengths of character as well as their weaknesses.

STRENGTHS

Moses

Moses is the dominant figure throughout the book. In many respects he was a prophet, a priest and a king.

We have seen already how other prophets were given visions and dreams, but Moses spoke face to face with God in the tabernacle. He was even allowed to see a part of God – he saw his 'back'.

He also acted in the role of priest. There are five occasions when he interceded with God. Indeed, on occasions he was quite bold in the way he prayed for the people and urged God to be true to himself.

He was never called 'king', and of course this was some centuries before the monarchy was established, but he led the people into battle and ruled over them, and so functioned as a king, even if the title was not used.

One of the most notable things about Moses was that when he was criticized, badly treated or betrayed he never tried to defend himself. Writing about himself, he says he was the meekest of all the men on the earth – a hard thing to say if you want it to remain true! Of course, Moses was saying no more than Jesus when he said we should learn from him for he was meek and humble. Moses let the Lord defend him. Meekness is not weakness, but it does mean not trying to defend yourself.

Aaron

Aaron was Moses' brother, assigned to Moses as his 'spokesman' when Moses had to face the Pharaoh in Egypt. He too was a prophet. He was also designated to be a priest, the chief priest. The Aaronic priesthood became the heart of the worship and ritual of the ancient people of God.

Miriam

Miriam was Moses' and Aaron's sister. She was known as a prophetess. She sang and danced with joy when the Egyptians were drowned in the sea.

So we have Moses as prophet, priest and king, Aaron as prophet and priest, and Miriam as prophetess. Note that the gifts are shared and that prophecy is a ministry for women as well as for men. Miriam's particular prophetic gift was expressed in song. There is a very direct link between prophecy and music. In later years King David chose choirmasters who were also prophets, and Ezekiel would often request music as a preparation for his prophesying. It seems that there is something about the right kind of music which releases the prophetic spirit.

Despite their strengths and gifts, however, each of these leaders failed in some way. It is instructive for us to examine their failings in detail.

WEAKNESSES

Miriam

Miriam's problem was jealousy: she desired honour for herself. She wanted to speak with God as Moses did. In addition she was critical of his choice of wife. Miriam was punished with 'leprosy' for seven days until she repented. She was among those who died at Kadesh.

Aaron

The next to drop out of the leadership picture was Aaron. Once again his problem was jealousy and desire for honour. Miriam and Aaron were together in criticizing Moses. Their excuse was that Moses had married someone of whom they did not approve (he married a Kushite woman who had come out of Egypt with them and who was not even a Hebrew). God did not criticize him for doing that, but Miriam and Aaron did.

Aaron thus died at Mount Hor, a little further on from Kadesh, when he was over 100 years old. Soon after they expressed jealousy and desire for honour, both Aaron and Miriam died.

Moses

Even Moses failed. He became very impatient with the people. The New Testament tells us that he put up with the people for 40 years in the wilderness. It was an amazing task of leadership to deal with over 2 million people who were always grumbling, complaining and having arguments that needed to be settled.

His big mistake came when he disobeyed God's instructions concerning the provision of water. Moses had provided water for the people by striking the rock with his rod. The limestone of the Sinai Desert has the peculiar property of holding reservoirs of water within itself. There are huge reserves of water in the Sinai Desert, but they are usually surrounded by rock and contained within the rock. Moses had released those reservoirs of water just by touching the rock with his rod.

On this second occasion when they were short of water God told Moses not to strike the rock but just to speak to it. A word would be sufficient to release the water in the rock. But Moses was so impatient with the people that he did not listen to God carefully and he struck the rock twice. God told Moses that because he was disobedient, he would not put a foot in the Promised Land. This is a poignant reminder of how important it is for a leader to listen carefully to God. Moses died at Mount Nebo in sight of the Promised Land, but unable to enter it.

Numbers tells us that it is a big responsibility to lead God's people. It must be done correctly and it must be done God's way.

Individuals

There were a number of individuals who let God down throughout the book of Numbers. The most outstanding was a man called Korah. We find Korah leading a rebellion because he was angry that the priesthood should be exclusively the right of Aaron and his family. Others joined him in this subversion, and soon there were 250 gathered together, challenging the authority of Moses and the priesthood of Aaron. The rebels said they could not believe that God had chosen Moses and Aaron and were critical of their failure to lead the Israelites into the Promised Land.

Then with great drama, Moses told the people to keep away from all the rebels' tents. Fire came down from heaven, struck their tents and destroyed them all. Korah saw it coming and ran away with a few of his followers, but they were swallowed up on some mudflats. (In the Sinai Desert there are mudflats which have a very hard crust but are very soft underneath, like thin ice on a pond. They are like a treacherous swamp or quicksand.)

Despite all this, some of the psalms are written by the sons of Korah. This man's family did not follow him in his rebellion, and his children later became singers in the temple. We do not need to follow our parents when they do evil.

Korah is mentioned in the book of Jude in the New Testament as a warning to Christians not to question God's appointments and become jealous.

Moses then announced that they needed to test whether God had chosen him and his brother for these positions. He told the leaders of the twelve tribes to get hold of twigs from the scrub bushes in the desert. They were to lay these twigs in the holy place before the Lord all night. In the morning Aaron's stick had blossomed with leaves, flowers and budding fruit. The other twigs were dead. From then on they put Aaron's rod inside the ark of the covenant as God's proof that Aaron was his choice and not self-appointed.

People

The people as a whole were problematic, as well as some individuals. Acts tells us that God *endured* their conduct for 40 years in the wilderness. Numbers says that the whole people failed except for two – two out of more than 2 million, not a high proportion. The people had one general problem and failed on three occasions of particular note.

GRUMBLING

The general problem with the people was 'grumbling'. You need no talent to grumble, you need no brains to grumble, you need no character to grumble, you need no self-denial to set up the grumbling business. It is one of the easiest things in the world to do.

The people thought that because God was in the tabernacle, he did not know what they said when they went to their own tents. What a big mistake! They grumbled about the lack of water, they grumbled about the monotonous food. It says they grumbled because they could not have garlic, onions, fish, cucumbers, melons and leeks as they had in Egypt. God heard their grumbling and responded accordingly. Soon he sent them quails to supplement their diet of manna – so many that they lay 1.5 metres thick, covering 12 square miles of ground! The people went out to gather the quail, but while they were still eating the meat, God struck them with a severe plague because they had rejected him.

Grumbling probably does more damage to the people of God than any other sin.

OASIS OF KADESH

The first particular occasion for failure was when they arrived at the last oasis, 66 miles south-west of the Dead Sea (today called Ain Qudeist) in the Negev Desert. They were told to send 12 spies, one from each tribe, to spy out the land and return to tell the whole camp what it was like. They spent 40 days in the south around Hebron and also travelled up to the far north, and they found it a very fertile land. But the conclusion of their report was negative. They spread the rumour that the land would devour them. They would rather go back to Egypt.

Two of the spies, Joshua and Caleb, said that God was with them and there was nothing to fear. They agreed that the land was well fortified and that it was inhabited by much bigger people. We know from archaeology that the average height of the Hebrew slaves was quite small compared to the Canaanites. They agreed too that the walls around the cities provided an obstacle. But they argued that God had not brought them this far to leave them in the desert. They told the people that God would carry them on his shoulders (just as a small boy might feel like a giant on the shoulders of his father).

The pessimistic arguments of the other 10 spies were more persuasive, however. The crowd actually wanted to stone Moses and Aaron for bringing them all this way. It had been just three months since they had left Egypt, but they were prepared to kill Moses and Aaron for bringing them out of slavery! They preferred to trust in what the 10 spies saw and said. They took the majority verdict, which in this case was contrary to God's intentions.

The contrast in the two reports is remarkable. The 10 men said they were not able to take the land and that was that; Joshua and Caleb said, 'We can't, but God can'. This was not merely positive thinking but a willingness to see the problems as opportunities for God.

As a result of the faithless outlook of the majority, God swore that not one of that generation would ever get into the Promised Land – except Joshua and Caleb. We are told that he swore by himself, because there is no one else higher by whom he could swear.

They had been spying out the land for 40 days, so God said that for every day they had spied out the land and come to the wrong conclusion, they would spend one year in the wilderness. He made the punishment fit the crime. This event becomes the hinge of the book of Numbers, just a third of the way through. Had they obeyed God, the rest of the events in the book would never have taken place.

THE VALLEY OF 'SCORPIONS'

The next time the people tested God and failed came after a magnificent victory over the Canaanite king of Arad.

They made their way back down into the deep valley of Arovar, also known as the 'valley of the scorpions'. It is just below Mount Hor and is well known for its scorpion and snake population. Once again the Israelites grumbled against God, returning to the theme of the poor diet, saying they would prefer to return to Egypt rather than remain in the desert.

This time God punished them by sending snakes so that many were bitten and died. Realizing their sin, they asked Moses to intercede for them. God did not stop the snakes, but he sent a cure for the snakebites. Moses set up a copper snake on a pole on the top of the mountain looking over the valley. If anyone was bitten by a snake, they could look at that copper snake on the pole and would not die. All they needed was faith to believe it would work.

PLAIN OF MOAB

The third and final crisis came when they got to the plains of Moab. They achieved a number of victories along the way. They wanted to use a main route through Edom. Their request was denied, despite their historical links (Edom was descended from Esau, Jacob's brother). A battle ensued and God gave them victory over Edom and Moab, so they were feeling confident. They camped by the Jordan looking across to the Promised Land.

But there was opposition to their advance on Canaan. The people of Ammon and Moab, owning land bordering the Promised Land, decided to disrupt their plans and hired a soothsayer from Syria to achieve their aim.

This soothsayer from Damascus was named Balaam. He had built a reputation for seeing the defeats of the armies he had cursed. But he had never been asked to curse Israel, for, as he actually explained to those who hired him, he could only say what God gave him to say! It was customary for a soothsayer to curse the opposition prior to a battle and so Balaam was asked to pronounce ill words upon the Israelites. His motive was purely the fee he would be paid. However, he proved to be unable to utter curses against Israel and ended up blessing her instead. He was unable to help himself!

Balaam announces that God will bless and multiply Israel – a prediction about King David and the son of David. So we have an amazing account of a non-believer prophesying a blessing upon Israel.

The account also tells the extraordinary story of the talking ass who refuses to advance when he sees an angel in his path. After Balaam beats the ass for refusing to move, the ass finally tells him why he is not moving! (Those who question whether this took place forget that animals can be possessed by evil spirits and good spirits. The serpent in the Garden of Eden and Jesus sending demons into the pigs are two biblical examples.) The message is clear: the animal has more sense than Balaam!

It is a sad story because of the sequel. Balaam finally realized how to obtain money from the kings of Ammon and Moab. He told them to forget about cursing but instead to send some of their pretty girls into the camp to seduce the Israelites. As this was prohibited by the law, most of the illicit sex took place outside the camp. But one man, Zimri, had the affront to bring a girl to the very door of the tabernacle.

Seeing this awful act, a man named Phinehas pinned the couple to the ground with a spear. Thereafter he was given a perpetual priesthood for himself and his family. He was the only man to defend God's house against what was happening in God's sight. The judgement may seem harsh, but remember that the Israelites were heading for the Promised Land. One of the worst features they would find there would be immorality. There were fertility goddesses, occult statues and phallic symbols, and all kinds of licentious behaviour. They needed to realize that such things were abominations before God.

What can we learn from Numbers?

Numbers was written for the Jews in order that later generations might learn to fear God. It was, therefore, written for Christians too, so that we might learn from their failures. We have seen already how Paul told the Corinthians that these events were recorded as 'examples', warning us not to live as the Israelites did. We can also fail to arrive, just as they did. The Bible is a mirror in which we see ourselves, according to James. We can live and die in the wilderness; we can look back on the 'pleasures of sin' but be unable to look forward to 'God's rest' in the Promised Land.

We can learn more about the character of God from Numbers, and the twin themes of kindness and sternness are taken up again at various times in the New Testament, in Romans, Hebrews, Jude and 2 Peter.

Jude also mentions both Korah and Balaam. Grumbling was as big a problem in the early Church as it was in Israel. When people grumble and complain it is called a 'bitter root' which can grow inside a fellowship and cause trouble.

In the New Testament we are reminded that we are names, not numbers. Even the hairs of our head are numbered. Our names are in the 'book of life', but there is also evidence that our names can be erased.

What Numbers says about God

In Numbers we are told very clearly that there are two sides to God's character. The apostle Paul draws them out when he says, 'Consider then the kindness and sternness of God...'

1. On the one hand we see his provision of food, drink, clothes and shoes. We see God providing his people with protection from their enemies, greater than them in size and number. We see his preservation of the nation despite their sinfulness.
2. On the other hand we see his justice. He is faithful to his covenant promises, punishing the people when they sin. This involves discipline, and ultimately disinheritance if they refuse to go on and follow his will.

We deal with the same God. He is holy and we must fear him.

What Numbers says about Jesus

1. As Israel went through the wilderness, so Jesus spent 40 days in the wilderness being tempted.
2. John 3:16 is well known, but the verse before it less so: '...as Moses lifted up the serpent in the wilderness, so must the son of man be lifted up.'
3. John also asserts that Jesus is the 'manna', the 'bread from heaven'.
4. Astonishingly, the apostle Paul speaks of the water being struck from the rock in the wilderness, suggesting that the rock was none other than Christ.
5. Hebrews says that if the ashes of a heifer could bring forgiveness, how much more will the blood of Christ achieve the same thing.

6. Perhaps the most amazing thing is that Balaam, the false prophet, actually made a true prophecy about Jesus! 'I see him, but not now; I behold him, but not near. A star will come out of Jacob; a sceptre will rise out of Israel.' From that time on, every devout Jew looked for the star of the king to come, and that is what led the wise men to Bethlehem.

Blessings of fellowship with God

Perhaps the best-known verse in Numbers is 6:24: 'The LORD bless you and keep you; the LORD make his face shine upon you and be gracious to you; the LORD turn his face towards you and give you peace.'

This was the blessing that God gave Aaron to give to the people when they set off from camp on the next part of their journey. It has every mark of direct inspiration from God because it is mathematically perfect. Whenever God speaks, his language is mathematically perfect. In the Hebrew there are three lines in the blessing:

> The LORD bless you and keep you
> The LORD make his face shine upon you and be gracious to you
> The LORD turn his face towards you and give you peace

In the Hebrew, there are 3 words in the first sentence, 5 in the second, and 7 in the third. There are 15 letters in the first, 20 in the second, and 25 in the third. There are 12 syllables in the first, 14 in the second, and 16 in the third. If you take the word 'LORD' out, you are left with 12 Hebrew words. We are left with the Lord and the 12 tribes of Israel! It is mathematically perfect. Even in English it builds up – there is a kind of crescendo through the lines. Each line has two verbs, and the second expands the first.

The blessing applies to Christians today, for the two thing the blessing offers are **grace** and **peace**. This is the Christian blessing given in every epistle in the New Testament: 'Grace and peace to you from God our Father and the Lord Jesus Christ.'

We too can receive the blessings of fellowship with God that Israel enjoyed – if we heed the lessons of Numbers.

PART V

DEUTERONOMY

Introduction

Every Jewish synagogue includes a large cupboard, usually covered with a curtain or a veil. Inside the cupboard are some scrolls wrapped in beautifully embroidered cloth. These scrolls are the law of Moses. They are called the Torah, which means 'instruction', and are regarded as foundational to the whole Old Testament. They are read through aloud once a year.

When a scroll was removed from the cupboard, the first part would be unrolled to reveal the opening words. The book became known by these words. The book of Deuteronomy is simply called 'The Words', because the first phrase in the Hebrew is 'These are the words'. When the Hebrew Old Testament was translated into Greek, they had to think of a more appropriate name. 'Deuteronomy' comes from two words in the Greek language, *deutero*, which means 'second', and *nomos*, which means 'law'.

The name gives us a clue to its content, for in Deuteronomy we find that the Ten Commandments appear again, just as in the book of Exodus.

A second reading

Why is it that the Ten Commandments need to be repeated a second time? Furthermore, there are 613 laws of Moses in total and they are all repeated. Why?

The clue lies in the book of Numbers. Deuteronomy was written 40 years after the book of Exodus. During those 40 years an entire generation died. These consisted of all the adults who came out of Egypt, crossed the Red Sea, camped at Sinai and heard the Ten Commandments the first time. By the time of Deuteronomy, they were all dead (with the exception of Moses, Joshua and Caleb). They had broken the law so quickly that God had said they would never get into the Promised Land. Their punishment was to wander around the wilderness for the 40 years until an entire generation had disappeared.

The new generation were only little children when they crossed the Red Sea and camped at Sinai. Most of them, therefore, would barely remember what had happened when their fathers came out of Egypt, and certainly would not recall the reading of the law at Sinai. So Moses read and explained the law a second time. Each generation must renew the covenant with God.

There is another reason for the second reading. This is to do with the timing. They were about to go into the Promised Land. They had been on their own in the wilderness and now they were facing a land that was already occupied by enemies. So the law was read and explained when the people were still on the east side of the River Jordan so that they might know what God required of them.

In addition, their leader Moses was not going to go in with them. He had forfeited his right to go in because he disobeyed God's Word concerning the provision of water from the rock. God had shown him that he was going to die in just seven days' time. So Moses wanted to ensure that this new generation w informed about the past and ready to face the future. Indeed they would see the miracle of the parting of the water all over again, this time with the River Jordan. God wanted them to know his miraculous power, just as the previous generation had done.

It is important that we are clear about the context in which the law was given for the second time. God brought the Israelites through the Red Sea first and then made the covenant at Sinai. He did not tell them how to live until he had saved them. This is a pattern throughout the whole Bible: God first of all shows us his grace by saving us, and then he explains how we should be living.

This new generation were going to see God rescue them and take them through the Jordan, which at that time of year was in flood and impassable. Having seen that miracle, they would go on to their own equivalent of Mount Sinai (Mount Ebal and Gerizim) and hear a repetition of the blessings and curses of the Lord. It was a repeat performance at the end of 40 years for an entirely new generation.

Deuteronomy therefore, the last of the books of Moses, is written and spoken in the Israelites' camp on the east side of the River Jordan, while Moses is still alive and still leading them.

Land

There are certain key phrases in the book of Deuteronomy. One occurs nearly 40 times. It is **'the land the LORD your God gives you'**. The Israelites are reminded that this land is a gift, an undeserved gift. Psalm 24 states that 'The earth is the LORD's, and everything in it.' When we argue about who has the ownership of land, we should remember that ultimately God owns it all. He gives it to whomever he wishes. In Acts 17

Paul, addressing the Athenians on Mars Hill, explained that it is God who decides how much space and how much time a nation has on this earth.

The second phrase which occurs the same number of times is 'go in and possess the land'. Everything we receive from God is a gift, but we have to take it. Salvation is a free gift from God, but we must 'go in and possess it' for it to be ours. God does not force it on us. Possessing the land would be a very costly thing for the Israelites: they would have to fight for it; they would have to struggle for it. Even though God gives everything to us, we have to make an effort to take it.

An important question arising from Deuteronomy concerns the ownership of the land. Was it to be theirs for ever, or was it theirs to keep or lose? There are two conclusions we can draw.

1. UNCONDITIONAL OWNERSHIP

God said he was giving the land to them *for ever*. This did not, however, mean they could necessarily *occupy* it for ever.

2. CONDITIONAL OCCUPATION

The occupation of the land was conditional. *Whether* they lived in it and enjoyed it depended on *how* they lived in it.

The Deuteronomy message is very simple: You can keep the land as long as you keep my law. If you do not keep my law, even though you own the land and I have given it to you, you will not be free to live in it and enjoy it.

There is a difference between 'unconditional ownership' and 'conditional occupation'. This distinction was one about which the prophets of the Old Testament needed to remind the people. The prophets could see that the people's behaviour would mean a forfeiture of their right to keep the land.

To this day the promises of God are conditional. They are gifts, but how we live in those promises determines whether we can enjoy them.

Covenant framework

The framework of covenant described in Deuteronomy was used throughout the ancient Near East. Whenever a king expanded his empire and conquered other countries he would make what was known as a 'suzerain treaty'. This was an agreement which in basic terms said that if the conquered behaved themselves, the king would protect them and provide for them, but if they misbehaved, he would punish them. Numerous examples of such treaties from the ancient world have been uncovered by archaeologists, particularly in Egypt. The pattern of the treaties is exactly the same in outline as the book of Deuteronomy.

Presumably Moses saw and studied these treaties when he was educated in Egypt. Moses presents the covenant to the people of Israel in the form of a treaty since the Lord was their king, and they were his subjects. The pattern of the suzerain treaty went as follows:

- **Preamble**: 'This is a treaty between Pharaoh and the Hittites...'
- **Historical prologue** summarizing how the king and his new subjects came to be related to each other
- **Declaration of the basic principles** on which the whole treaty would be based
- **Detailed laws** as to how the subjects were to behave
- **Sanctions** (i.e. rewards or punishments): what the king would do if they did behave properly, and what he would do if they did not

- **Witnessed signature**, normally calling on 'the gods' to witness the treaty
- **Provision for continuity**: what would happen if the king died and naming a successor to whom the people would still be subject

All would be settled in a ceremony when the treaty would be written down, signed and agreed by the king and his new subjects.

It is easy to see the parallels between this form and the form and content of the law given in Deuteronomy:

- **Preamble**   1:1–5
- **Historical prologue**   1:6–4:49
- **Declaration of basic principles**   5–11
- **Detailed laws**   12–26
- **Sanctions**   27–28
- **Invocation of divine witness**   30:19; 31:19; 32
- **Provision for continuity**   31–34

The sanctions are a key part of the book and concern our understanding of later events in biblical history. There were two things that God would do in terms of sanctions if the Israelites did not live the way he told them to.

NATURAL SANCTIONS

The natural sanction he could impose was the absence of rain. The land they were entering was between the Mediterranean Sea and the Arabian desert. When the wind blew from the west it would pick up rain from the Mediterranean and drop it on the Promised Land. But if the wind came from the east, it would be the dry, hot desert wind which dries up everything and turns the land into a place of desolation. During Elijah's day, therefore, God punished the idolatry of the people with a drought for three and a half years. This was a simple way of God rewarding or punishing the people.

MILITARY SANCTIONS

If the natural sanction failed, he would move on to something rather more fierce. He would use human agents to attack them. Amos 9 tells us something very significant in this regard. We read that when Israel was crossing the Jordan, God brought another people at the same time into the same land from the west. These people were called Philistines. Thus God brought a people who proved to be Israel's greatest enemy into the same land at the same time. Israel settled in the hills and the Philistines on the coastal plain (now the Gaza Strip). If Israel were faithful in keeping the laws they would enjoy peace. If they misbehaved God would send the Philistines to deal with them. It was as simple as that.

Corruption

The land of Canaan was inhabited by a mixture of Amorites and Canaanites. God told the Israelites to drive out these nations and possess the land. This point has given rise to a common objection to the Bible. Such apparent genocide seems barbaric to the modern mind. How can we reconcile a God of love with a God who tells the Jews to slaughter all the people living in the Promised Land? It seems immoral and unjust.

The answer is found back in Genesis. God told Abraham that he would keep his family and their descendants in a foreign country for 400 years until the wickedness of the Amorites was complete. God actually waited 400 years for those people to become so bad that they no longer deserved to live in Canaan – because they did not deserve to live anywhere on his earth. God does not allow people to go on occupying his earth regardless of what they do. He is very patient with them, but eventually he will act in judgement. Archaeology has revealed evidence of just how wicked the Amorites were. Sexually transmitted diseases were commonplace amongst them, for example. If the Israelites had mixed with these people it would have been like living in a land where everybody had AIDS, quite apart from the generally unhealthy influence of their corrupt lifestyle.

In Deuteronomy God says, 'It is not because of your righteousness or your integrity that you are going in to take possession of their land; but on account of the wickedness of these nations, the LORD your God will drive them out before you, to accomplish what he swore to your forefathers, to Abraham, Isaac and Jacob.'

Some ask why it was necessary for the *Israelites* to slaughter them. Could God not have destroyed them himself? The answer is very clear. He needed to teach the Israelites the importance of living the way he said. If they behaved like the Amorites, they would go exactly the same way.

When we read Deuteronomy we must realize that we are reading a *mirror image* of life in Canaan. Everything God tells the Israelites not to do is what was already happening in Canaan. We can build up a picture of what was happening in the Promised Land before they got into it. This can be summarized in three words.

1. IMMORALITY

We have noted already that there were sexually transmitted diseases in the land. There was fornication, adultery, incest, homosexuality, transvestism and buggery. There was also widespread divorce and remarriage. Deuteronomy outlines how all such behaviour was strictly prohibited.

2. INJUSTICE

Deuteronomy also addresses injustice. 'The rich were getting richer and the poorer getting poorer.' The age-old sins of pride, greed and selfishness were evident, leading to exploitation of the poor. Those with disabilities, the blind, the deaf, were not cared for. Many people were unable to break the shackles of poverty caused by usury. God said the Israelites were to be selfless. They were to look after the deaf, the blind, the widow and the orphan. People mattered.

3. IDOLATRY

Canaan was full of idolatry. There was occultism, superstition, astrology, spiritism, necromancy, and fertility cults. They worshipped 'Mother Earth', believing that sexual acts had links with the fertility of the land. In the pagan temples there were male and female prostitutes, and worship included sex. These practices were reflected in the monuments throughout the land: *asherah* poles (phallic symbols) were frequently seen on the hills as a witness to the pagan rituals which predominated.

Deuteronomy makes it clear how God viewed such behaviour. It was his land and it was now totally corrupt, defiled, debased. It was disgraced and God could not let it go on. Are things so different now?

The last work of Moses

Deuteronomy is the last of the five books of Moses, the Pentateuch. We have seen that it was written at a critical moment for the people of Israel. They were about to enter the Promised Land, but Moses was not going to lead them. He was by then an old man of 120, and was entering his last week of life (the book ends with his death). Having seen the weakness of the present generation's parents, he was afraid that they might go the same way. He saw ahead to the battles they would need to fight, both physical and spiritual.

In the last week of his life he spoke three times to them. The whole of Deuteronomy is made up of three long speeches, each of which must have taken the best part of a day to give. This spoken style comes across. It is a very personal and emotional book. Moses is appealing to the people, like a dying father to his children.

It is quite likely that during these last six days of the last week in Moses' life he spoke and wrote on alternate days. On days 1, 3 and 5 he gave these discourses, then on days 2, 4 and 6 he wrote down what he had said the previous day. He handed what he wrote to the priests, who placed it alongside the ark of the covenant, so that the people would never forget. This is his 'last will and testament', the greatest prophet of the Old Testament bringing the Word of the Lord to his people.

The book can be neatly divided into the three parts.

1. Past: Recollection (1:1–4:43)
a. faithlessness condemned (1:6–3:29)
b. faithfulness counselled (4:1–43)

2. Present: Regulation (4:44–26:19)
a. love expressed (4:44–11:32)
b. law expanded (12:1–26:19)

3. Future: Retribution (27:1–34:12)
a. covenant affirmed (27:1–30:20)
b. continuity assured (31:1–34:12)

First Discourse (1:1–4:43) Past

In the first discourse, Moses looks back to the days after Sinai when God had made the covenant with his listeners' parents. He reminds them that although it only takes 11 days to walk from Sinai to the Promised Land, their parents took 13,780. When they arrived at Kadesh Barnea on the border, they paused and at God's instruction sent one man from each of the tribes to spy out the land. The spies were positive about the quality of food in the land, but not about their chances of conquering it. The people were too big and the towns impregnable, they said. Only two, Joshua and Caleb, urged the people to trust God and go on.

Israel had everything in front of them and yet their morale failed. Although God had been faithful to them, they were faithless. The message of Chapter 4 is simply this: 'Do not be like your parents. They lost their faith and they lost the land. If you keep yours, you can keep the land.'

Second Discourse (4:44–26:19) Present

The legislation in the second part is not as easy to read. It is by far the longest section, probably given on the third day of that last week in Moses' life. It outlines the way the Israelites must live if they are to remain in the land God is giving them.

Summary

Chapter 5 Moses begins with the basic principles of God's righteous way of living, his upright way of living, namely the Ten Commandments. These are all about one thing, *respect*. Respect God, respect his name, respect his day, respect your parents, respect life, respect marriage, respect property, respect people's reputation. The quickest way to destroy society is to destroy respect.

It is very interesting to draw a contrast between the law of Moses and the laws in pagan society. If you contrast the standards in Moses' law with the worst practices of pagan society, as we have already done with the Amorites in Canaan, it is obvious what a pure, holy law is given in the Ten Commandments.

Chapter 6 The covenant law is expounded and expanded. We are told the *purpose* for the law: it is so that love can be communicated from one generation to the next.

Chapter 7 They are commanded to abolish all idolatry (i.e. the First Commandment) and exterminate the Canaanites, that they may not be led astray.

Chapter 8 They are encouraged to remember with gratitude God's dealings with his people. They are warned not to forget, especially when prosperity comes.

9:1–10:11 Moses reviews the sin and rebelliousness of the people. They are warned not to become self-righteous.

10:12–11:33 The theme in this section is obedience. If they are obedient they will be blessed; if they are disobedient they will be cursed – the choice is theirs. This is an emphasis throughout the book. The word 'hear' comes 50 times and the words 'do', 'keep' and 'observe' 177 times.

Alongside this, it is important to know that another common word in Moses' exposition is 'love'. It is used 31 times. If you love the Lord you keep his laws. In the New Testament Paul says that love is the fulfilling of the law. It is not a matter of legalism, but a matter of love. To love is to obey, because in God's sight love is loyalty. It means staying true to someone. Love and law are not opposed to one another – they stand together.

Chapters 12–26 A huge amount is covered in these chapters, sometimes in amazing detail. In this section of his speech Moses passes from the general to the particular, from the vertical (our relationship with God) to the horizontal (our relationship with others).

Contrasting standards

We can best observe these laws against a background of contrasts. What was so different, so special, about the law of Moses compared to other societies in the region?

1. STANDARDS IN THE PROMISED LAND

We have already seen how the laws in Deuteronomy are a *mirror image* of what was taking place in the land at that time. Some of the more puzzling laws relate to the practices of those already occupying the land.

2. STANDARDS IN NEIGHBOURING LANDS

There is also an interesting comparison to be made between the law of Moses and another law which has been discovered from the ancient world, the code of Hammurabi, an ancient Amorite King of Babylon (or Babel). These laws were written 300 years before Moses. They include prohibitions on killing, adultery, stealing and false witness. Furthermore, the famous law of *lex talionis*, or the law of revenge ('an eye for an eye and a tooth for a tooth'), is also included. All this should not surprise us. In Romans the apostle Paul says that God 'has written his law on the hearts' of pagans. He did not just write it on stone –

he has written it into the hearts of people so that everyone knows that certain things are wrong. For example, every society in the world has always thought incest was wrong.

There are, however, some big differences between Hammurabi's law and the law of Moses. There was just one punishment for any wrong done, and that was death. In the law of Moses the death penalty is quite rare. There are only 18 things in the law of Moses that deserve the death penalty. By comparison to Hammurabi's law, the law of Moses is not nearly so harsh.

Another huge difference is that in the law of Moses slaves and women are treated as people, whereas in the law of Hammurabi they are treated as property. Women have none of the rights and respect in the law of Hammurabi that they possess in the law of Moses.

The law of Hammurabi also includes class distinctions. There are nobles and common people, and a different law applies depending on the class. In the law of Moses there is no such thing as class. The same law applies to everybody.

A final point to note is that the laws of Hammurabi are *casuistic* laws – they are presented in the form of conditions. '*If* you do this, *then* you must die.' The laws of Moses are presented in what is called an *apodeictic* manner – not as conditions, but as commands. 'You *must not* do this.' The laws of Moses reflect God's right as king to say what should be. He makes commands because he sets the standard.

The commands and legislation fall into a number of different categories, detailed in the following sections.*

---

* For the following classification of the Mosaic laws I am indebted to my friend F. LaGard Smith, Professor of Law in Pepperdine University, Malibu, California, who has produced the New International Version without chapter and verse numbers, with the books in chronological order and with the laws arranged in convenient categories, as here. The hardback is entitled *The Narrated Bible* and the paperback *The Daily Bible* (both Harvest House, 1978).

1. Religious/ceremonial

IDOLATRY/PAGANISM

■ Israel is forbidden to follow other gods, or erect graven images. We are told that the Lord is a jealous God. Jealousy is an appropriate emotion for God, even if we might not think so at first. We are jealous when we want what is ours. Envy is when we want what is *not* ours. So just as it would be appropriate for a man to be jealous if another man took his wife, it is right that God should be jealous for his people when they follow other gods.

■ As a consequence of the First Commandment, *asherah* poles are specifically forbidden.

■ There are laws about cutting flesh and shaving heads when mourning.

■ If a relative seeks to entice their family away from the worship of God, they must be put to death – there should be no mercy.

■ When attacking idolatrous cities the Israelites are told to kill all the people and burn the city so that it could never be rebuilt.

■ Idolaters are to be stoned on the word of two or three witnesses, one of whom should be responsible for casting the first stone.

■ There is to be one place of worship. All 'high places' where the Canaanites worship are to be destroyed.

■ The Israelites are not to enquire about or get interested in other religions. They must shun child sacrifice, which is detestable.

FALSE SPIRITUALISTS

■ All false prophets, dreamers, and those who 'follow other gods' are to be put to death.

- All forms of spiritualism are punishable by death: consulting the dead, witchcraft, omens, spells, mediums.
- We are told that a true prophet like Moses will be raised up (a reference to Jesus).
- When false prophets speak in the name of other gods, or when they speak but the prophecy does not come true, they are to be put to death.

BLASPHEMY

- If the name of God is misused, the miscreant must be put to death.

DEDICATIONS

- All first-born animals must be dedicated to the Lord.

TITHING

- A tenth of all produce is to be set aside. Every three years produce would be passed on for the Levites, aliens, fatherless and widows.

CONQUEST

- Baskets of firstfruits are to be offered from any land the Israelites conquer.
- They are to declare their history when they arrive in the land, recounting their rescue from Egypt.
- Prayers of thanksgiving are also to be made.

SABBATH

- Up until the time of Moses, nobody had a Sabbath. It is a new provision for slaves who have previously worked seven days a week, but who are now given one day a week free from work.

FEASTS (ALL PILGRIM EVENTS)

- Passover.
- Weeks (Pentecost).
- Tabernacles.

SACRIFICES AND OFFERINGS

- If there is a murder, and the perpetrator cannot be found, a heifer is to be sacrificed to declare the innocence of the community.

EXCLUSIONS FROM THE ASSEMBLY

- Those with mutilated or castrated genitals are excluded from the assembly of the Lord.
- Children of forbidden unions (up to the tenth generation) are also forbidden to enter.
- Ammonites and Moabites are explicitly forbidden.
- Edomites (from the third generation) are permitted to enter.

VOWS

- Whatever we vow we must do. Vows are freely made, so should be followed through. If you make a vow to God you must keep it.

SEPARATION

- No mixing of seeds is allowed.
- A donkey and an ox should not be yoked together.
- Clothes of wool and linen may not be mixed.

These laws of separation may seem very strange, but they were connected to the old fertility cult which was widespread in the land. The pagans believed that by mixing such things they were producing fertility. God was emphasizing that *he* gives fertility: they did not need to practise such superstition.

2. Government

KING

There are laws here for a king, even though they were not to have a king for centuries.

- God is their king – kingship is a concession, not part of his plan.
- When a king comes to the throne he has to write out the laws of Moses in his own handwriting and read them regularly.
- The king is instructed not to have many wives, many horses, or much money.

JUDGES

- Rules for conducting law courts are given, including provision for a court of appeal. Interestingly, the penalty for contempt of court given here is death.
- There are also rules for justice: no bribes and no favouritism. An alien, an orphan and a widow must get exactly the same treatment as the richest businessman.
- There must be at least two or three witnesses who agree totally on what they have seen or heard. If they bear false witness they must suffer exactly what the person would have suffered if they were found guilty. If my false testimony in court gets someone fined £1,000, then when I am discovered to be a false witness I am fined £1,000. 'An eye for an eye, a tooth for a tooth.'
- There are regulations covering the administration of punishments. Floggings are to be a maximum of 40 strokes (they usually made it 39 to make quite sure they did not break the law). Excessive flogging is dehumanizing – the criminal is treated like a lump of meat. When a person is executed, the

body must not be left hanging on the tree after sunset. (The apostle Paul applies that to Jesus on the cross in Galatians 3.) There is no imprisonment.

3. Special crimes

AGAINST PERSONS

- Murder always carries the death penalty, unless it was manslaughter and unintended. Six cities of refuge, three either side of the Jordan, are to be set up where a man who has killed accidentally can run to escape the death penalty.
- Kidnapping also carries the death penalty.
- Death is the penalty for rapists if the attack took place in the country, but both parties are to be put to death if the attack took place in the town, because the victim could have cried out.

AGAINST PROPERTY

- There are laws against theft and the removing of boundary markers around land.

4. Personal rights and responsibilities

- Injuries and damages.
- Masters and servants: slaves have rights; workers should be paid on time.
- Credit, interest and collateral. Debts are to be cancelled after seven years by every creditor cancelling loans made to fellow Israelites. Interest must not be charged.
- Weights and measures. Properly weighted scales are to be used at all times.
- Inheritance. It is the responsibility of the next of kin to continue the family line.

5. Sexual relations

- Marriage. Strict instructions concerning the marriage bond, for those married, those pledged to be married, and those raped.
- Divorce. Divorce on the grounds of the husband 'disliking' his wife is prohibited. Remarriage to the original husband following a divorce is forbidden to protect the innocent woman.
- Adultery. Both parties should be put to death.
- Transvestism. Cross-dressing is detestable to God.

6. Health

- For leprosy there is a careful procedure to follow if anyone suspects they may have the disease, involving examination by the priest.
- There are laws against eating animals that are found dead.
- Strict rules govern 'clean and unclean food'. Camels, rabbits, pigs and certain birds must not appear on the menu.
- Meat and milk are not to be cooked together.

This last point is a law which has been misunderstood by almost every Jew: 'You shall not boil a kid in its mother's milk.' On the basis of this one verse the Jews have erected a 'kosher' system of diet whereby they have (effectively) two kitchens with two completely different sets of pots and pans and sinks to wash them in – in order that dairy products are kept separate from meat products, which Abraham never did, offering veal and butter to his visitors. They have totally misunderstood the purpose of the law, which once again was connected to a rite of the pagan fertility cult. The Canaanites believed that cooking a kid in its mother's milk caused it to have incest with its mother, which then promoted fertility.

7. Welfare

- Benevolence is not just encouraged, it is commanded. Sheaves of corn are to be left in the corner of the field for the poor to pick up.
- Parents should expect respect and support from their children: a stubborn, rebellious son is to be put to death.
- Neighbours whose animals have strayed are to be assisted.
- Animals are to be treated well: no one should muzzle an ox when it is treading out grain; it is permitted to take birds' eggs from the nest, but the mother should not be removed – she is to be left so that she can lay some more eggs.

8. Warfare

- Preparation is vital. War is not for the faint-hearted. Those afraid can go home.
- During a siege the soldiers must not cut down the trees around a city.
- A toilet area should be set up outside the camp and all waste covered up.
- A soldier who has recently been married can stay at home for a year before he has to go to war again. No one should go to war at the expense of a marriage at home.

What are we to make of all this?

1. SCOPE

God is interested in the whole of our lives. Living right is not just what you do in church on Sunday but concerns the whole of life. There is a right way to do everything. God wants people to be right in every area of their lives.

2. INTEGRATION

These laws show an amazing integration. We move, say, from a law about not eating camels to a law about observing a feast day. This is not pleasing to the modern western mind. We feel we must somehow classify all these laws. But God is saying that there is no division in life – there is no sacred/secular divide; all of life is for God.

3. PURPOSE

There is a clear purpose for all these laws. It was not to spoil the people's fun, or to hedge them about with restrictions. A recurrent phrase throughout the book is **'that it may be well with you and that you may live a long life in the land'**. God wants us healthy and happy, so he gave us laws. Some people picture God sitting in heaven saying 'don't' and 'thou shalt not'. But his purpose for prohibition is always for our good. He is concerned for our 'welfare'.

Third Discourse (27:1–34:12) Future

The third and last discourse given by Moses is in two parts.

1. Covenant affirmed (27:1–30:20)

In the first part he tells the Israelites that they are to ratify the law for themselves. After crossing the Jordan they are to stand on Mount Ebal and Mount Gerizim. The mountains are directly next to each other and form an amphitheatre with the valley in between. The people are to shout the blessings from Mount Gerizim and the curses from Mount Ebal. After each sentence they are to respond with an 'amen' – i.e. 'this is certain!' These curses and blessings are all included in Deuteronomy 28 (and, incidentally, in the Anglican Book of Common Prayer, to be recited every Lent).

Words are powerful. The rest of the history of the Old Testament hinges on Israel's response to these blessings and

curses. When we read Deuteronomy 28, it is like reading the whole history of Israel for the last 4,000 years.

2. Continuity assured (31:1–34:12)

Joshua is appointed as Moses' successor at the age of 80. Moses then gives the written law to priests, who place it beside the ark. He commands that the whole law be recited every seven years.

Moses finishes his message with a song. Like many prophets he was also a musician. His sister Miriam sang following the crossing of the Sea of Reeds, and now Moses recites the words of a song before his death. The song details the faithfulness of God and his just dealings with Israel. He is a rock, utterly dependable, unchangeable, totally reliable. After the song is finished, Moses blesses the 12 tribes and includes prophetic glimpses into the future.

Finally comes the death and burial of Moses – the only part of the five books of Moses that he did not write! Presumably Joshua added the details. Moses died alone, with his back against the rock on the top of Mount Nebo, looking across the Jordan to the land that had been promised, but in which he would never set foot.

Centuries later, we read in the Gospels that Moses spoke with Jesus on top of one of the mountains, but he never entered Canaan in his earthly life. He was also buried on Mount Nebo, though not by his fellow people. In the New Testament Jude tells us that an angel came to bury him. When the angel got to Moses, the devil was standing on the other side of him. The devil pointed out that this man was his because he had murdered an Egyptian. But the archangel Michael said to the devil, 'The Lord rebuke you!' and so Moses was buried by the angel. It was an amazing end to an amazing life. The people mourned him for one month before preparing to cross the River Jordan.

The importance of Deuteronomy

Deuteronomy is the key to the whole history of Israel. Unable and unwilling to expel the Canaanites from the land when they first arrived, very soon they had intermarried and were involved in the same evil practices as the pagans. In fact it took them a thousand years, from the time of Abraham to the time of David, finally to inhabit the land promised to them. In the following 500 years they lost it all, as we shall see in the book of Kings. The whole history of Israel can be summarized in just two sentences. Obedience and righteousness brought them blessing. Disobedience and wickedness brought them curses. All this is made abundantly clear in the book of Deuteronomy.

Deuteronomy plays a huge part in the New Testament too. It is quoted 80 times in just 27 books.

Jesus

- Jesus was *the* prophet foretold by Moses in Deuteronomy.
- Jesus knew Deuteronomy very well. When he was tempted in the wilderness he used the Scriptures to defend himself, and each time he quoted from Deuteronomy.
- In the Sermon on the Mount we are told that not 'one jot or tittle' will pass from the law.
- When Jesus was asked to summarize the law of Moses, he summarized it in words from Deuteronomy: 'Love the LORD your God with all your heart and soul and mind and strength,' and Leviticus: 'Love your neighbour as yourself.'

Paul

- Paul used Deuteronomy when he wrote about the importance of our hearts being changed.
- He used Jesus' death as an example of one who was cursed.

■ He quotes the law about muzzling the ox as a principle to be applied when supporting preachers.

Christians and Moses' law

How, then, should Christians today read the law of Moses?

Particular precepts

We are not under the law of Moses, but under the law of Christ. We need to find out, therefore, whether each Old Testament law is repeated or reinterpreted in the New Testament.

For example, out of the Ten Commandments, only the Fourth concerning the Sabbath is not repeated in the New Testament. And tithes are not enforced in the New Testament either, although we are encouraged to give generously, cheerfully and liberally. Laws about clean and unclean food are abolished.

General principles

We are saved *for* righteousness not *by* righteousness. This is an important concept to grasp. The need 'to do' is just as common in the New Testament as in the Old, but the motivation is also all-important now. Our righteousness must 'exceed that of the Pharisees and the scribes', but now our righteousness is *inward* as well as outward. Now we have the Spirit to enable us. Thus we are justified by faith, but judged by works.

It is worth noting, too, that Deuteronomy is a warning against syncretism. We can easily incorporate pagan practices into our lives without realizing it. Hallowe'en and Christmas, for instance, were originally both pagan festivals, which the Church sought to 'make Christian' when they should have avoided them altogether.

Conclusion

Deuteronomy is a crucial book within Israel's history, and not just because it was one of the five books of Moses. It reminds people of the past, teaches them how to live in the present, and urges them to look ahead to the future. It reflects Moses' concern that his people should not go astray. At the same time it states God's desire that his people, by honouring and respecting him, should be worthy of the land he was giving them.